PRAISE FOR

Diving in the Inner Ocean

"I am delighted that Dominic Liber has written this book. As a teacher of the Enneagram, students often ask me what to *do* with the knowledge they acquire. And my response is that without *practice,* such learning cannot take us very far. But here, in *Diving in the Inner Ocean*, Dominic has provided a beautifully written, lucid, and friendly introduction to what I see as the central practice for working with our personality and for exploring the deeper mysteries of our essential nature—the practice of inquiry. This book guides us step by step into developing the tools and capacities for inquiry, and whether you are an experienced meditator or are new to inner work, the teachings here are a treasure trove of helpful experience and insight. I enthusiastically recommend this book."

—RUSS HUDSON, author of *The Enneagram: Nine Gateways to Presence* and coauthor of *The Wisdom of the Enneagram*

"The cosmic ocean of consciousness is such a magnificent vastness— but where to begin? Are you sitting at the shore longing for a way in? Or adrift with only a memory of a rogue wave that grabbed you only to deposit you back on the sand, helpless to find your way back? Do you think the ocean of consciousness is just one thing and miss the riches it holds?

With his friendly, encouraging guidance, Dominic illuminates the way to inner exploration with a heart of adventure and the wisdom of a seasoned diver. The pages drip with the presence of the sea as he sharpens our diamond inquiry skill with the innate inner resources that have all but been forgotten. He deftly points us toward the numinous presences of strength, kindness, and steadfastness and sets our curiosity free to explore uncharted waters—all of it—the sparkling, the turbulent, the surface, and the depth. He leaves no shell unturned. Better yet, you will discover all of the magical treasures hidden within each one.

Dominic offers an invitation to return to our natural condition as part of that vast sea. You are fluid as an octopus and bright as the bioluminescence that lives at the mysterious depths.

Come on in! The conditions are perfect for a dive!"

—KAREN JOHNSON, cofounder of the Diamond Approach, author of *The Jeweled Path*, and coauthor of *The Power of Divine Eros*

"A brilliant, welcoming gift to the whole world. Dominic Liber lays out a lucid, warm path for becoming competent in an essential skill, diamond inquiry: a contemporary method for uncovering and manifesting our true nature. His work is kind and accompanied in every step with practices, warnings of pitfalls, and pre-forgiveness for any mistakes. Anyone seeking a direct experience of their authentic self will be well served by this compassionate, deeply human, and generous teaching."

—JAMES FLAHERTY, MCC, author of *Coaching: Evoking Excellence in Others* and founder of New Ventures West and Integral Coaching™

"Dominic's book elucidating the revolutionary practice of inquiry as practiced in the Diamond Approach path is excellent. The process of inquiry allows us to penetrate through our egoic experience and discover the treasures that lie beyond, and is a game-changing innovation in spiritual technology. With clarity and simplicity, he shows us how to navigate our inner life, likening it to learning how to skillfully scuba dive. The analogy of learning to dive into the ocean that he follows throughout is an apt one. He teaches us how to move beneath the surface of our experience and explore what underlies it. As our acclimation to our inner ocean deepens and we become more comfortable, he takes us into the depths of what's possible for us as human beings to experience. Not only descriptive but filled with exercises for the reader to practice, it is essential for those new to inquiry and a great enhancement for those already familiar with it."

—SANDRA MAITRI, author of *The Spiritual Dimension of the Enneagram* and *The Enneagram of Passions and Virtues*

DIVING
in the
INNER OCEAN

AN INTRODUCTION TO
PERSONAL TRANSFORMATION
THROUGH DIAMOND INQUIRY

Dominic C. Liber

FOREWORD BY A. H. ALMAAS

SHAMBHALA

Shambhala Publications, Inc.
2129 13th Street
Boulder, Colorado 80302
www.shambhala.com

Cover photo: Wonderful Nature/Shutterstock; Zakharchuk/Shutterstock
Cover design: Shubhani Sarkar
Interior design: Kate Huber-Parker

9 8 7 6 5 4 3 2 1

First Edition
Printed in the United States of America

♾ This edition is printed on acid-free paper that meets the
American National Standards Institute Z39.48 Standard.
♻ This book is printed on 30% postconsumer recycled paper.
For more information please visit www.shambhala.com.

Shambhala Publications is distributed worldwide by
Penguin Random House, Inc., and its subsidiaries.

LIBRARY OF CONGRESS CATALOGING-IN-PUBLICATION DATA
Names: Liber, Dominic C., author.
Title: Diving in the inner ocean: an introduction to personal transformation
through diamond inquiry / Dominic C. Liber; foreword by A. H. Almaas.
Description: First edition. | Boulder, Colorado: Shambhala, [2021] |
Includes bibliographical references and index.
Identifiers: LCCN 2020037481 | ISBN 9781611809084 (trade paperback)
Subjects: LCSH: Spiritual life—Ridhwan Foundation. |
Ridhwan Foundation—Doctrines.
Classification: LCC BP605.R53 L53 2021 | DDC 204—dc23
LC record available at https://lccn.loc.gov/2020037481

To all the teachers from whom I learn to inquire
The Guidance of Being
The originators of the Diamond Approach
Hameed Ali (A. H. Almaas) and Karen Johnson

My big group teachers over the years including
Bob Ball, John Davis, Jeanne Haye, Linda Krier,
Rennie Moran, Patty Rice

My private session teacher
Gina Crago

My mentor
Tejo Jourdan

&

To my own students
with whom I discover
often through trial and error
what helps them learn to inquire

CONTENTS

FOREWORD

A. H. Almaas

In this book, Dominic introduces and elucidates the practice of *diamond inquiry*, the primary practice of the teaching of the Diamond Approach. While central in this teaching, the practice can be useful in whatever path you happen to be on. Diamond inquiry is handy even if you are not on any spiritual path or engaged in any practice, because it clarifies what you experience and connects you to deeper strata of what you are. It takes you to greater intimacy with your subjectivity and gives you greater freedom in what you experience and how to live it. It helps to liberate you from many of your emotional or mental patterns that trap you in suffering or limit your life.

In a simple and easily accessible way, Dominic presents the practice of diamond inquiry that is the Diamond Approach's main contribution to spiritual practice. The Diamond Approach is a wide and deep teaching, with many facets and dimensions. It is a path of liberation from unnecessary baggage and of realization of what we truly are. The totality of this teaching can be discovered and experienced most easily through this practice of diamond inquiry. The path uses other practices, such as meditation of different kinds, a few of which are presented here. But I have found the inquiry that has developed within this path to be the most effective and efficient way to discover the truths revealed by this teaching. These are the truths of what we are, our true being and the being of all and everything. The path is not simply liberation but the discovery of the secrets of existence, the meaning of life, and so on. To traverse this path is to embark on an adventure of discovery, of discovering the inner or spiritual universe and its relation to our everyday reality.

The practice of diamond inquiry that developed in this path is not what most people think of or know as inquiry. It is not exactly scientific inquiry. It is not philosophic, mental, or even emotional inquiry, and it is not just psychological exploration. It is all of those but none of them. It is a kind of Socratic inquiry, but more personal and immediate in the here and now. The practice includes the psychological, scientific, and philosophical insights that have developed since the time of Socrates, but all within an exploration into the immediacy of our present experience. It is always relevant because it examines what we personally experience. So it is an inquiry that uses many of the spiritual elements and insights of our true being, but to see the meaning of what is now occurring in our immediate personal experience.

Why does this immediate personal experience matter? This might be an important question for you if you are following another spiritual path or engaging in a certain spiritual practice.

Most teachings recognize that fundamentally we are each whole, and we are all one. We discover this in time in our practice or path. But we tend not to consider this truth and its implications from the beginning of the path. If we believe that reality is one, why do we not generally consider (at least at first) that our spiritual depth and ordinary experience are one? Oneness means that everything in each of us is interconnected to everything else in us, at all psychological and spiritual levels. Yet most teachings do not address present-centered ordinary experience, except maybe in being aware of it, mindful of it, or witnessing it. Most spiritual teachings do not work on understanding this experience. Many of them even use practices that sidestep such experience; they go around it or try to go beyond it, as if the spiritual truth is not there in the ordinary present experience. However, this does not consider that the present experience, regardless of how ordinary and unspiritual it might at first appear to be, is intimately connected to everything in us, for we are fundamentally and ultimately whole and one with everything else.

The practice of diamond inquiry presented here is based on this fundamental truth—that whatever experience we have at the moment is inherently connected to our inner depths, but we simply do not see or recognize that. If we understand our everyday ordinary experience more fully than we do at first, it can lead us to hidden dimensions. In other words, by knowing experientially where we are in the present moment in our inner world more completely, we can see how it is connected to deeper meanings. Such dimensions appear through us understanding, by intimate feeling, what ordinarily arises in our present everyday experience. Our everyday experience can become an entry into deeper parts of who we are and a portal to the hidden truths of presence and even the transcendental levels of spirit.

Even though it is the primary practice in the Diamond Approach, it might become only an adjunct practice for you, complementing whatever spiritual practice you are engaging by helping you make sense of your ordinary experience in the light of spiritual realization. It has the potential of integrating your ordinary experience with the transcendent and timeless truths of spirit and being, helping you live your spiritual illumination, instead of it remaining only as an inner experience.

Dominic is quite eloquent in his illustration of the practice, and very helpful by the many examples and questions he presents to you. By encouraging you to remain with your experience, whatever it is, he takes you gently and gradually to deeper levels of your psyche and finally to the very presence of your spiritual nature. And he does it with simple, easy-to-understand language and metaphors. In my book *Spacecruiser Inquiry*, I presented the same practice, but my book turned out to be less accessible, regardless of its depth. Dominic's presentation is approachable, readily understood and integrated. It is a very good guide to such deep and effective practice. In simple and easy steps, he invites us to befriend our experience and to gently explore it through to its underlying meanings, coming to depths we have not contemplated and places we have not known in us. Before you know it, you learn how to navigate your experience and ride it to the deeper dimensions of who you are, with greater ease and freedom.

INTRODUCTION

SCUBA DIVING FOR THE SOUL

A late summer afternoon on a quietish Ibiza beach. Mellow beats drift across from a friend DJ-ing at a bar some way off. His partner is telling me about a new hobby: scuba diving! He lights up like a Christmas tree, animated with delight and wonder at his discovery. He is astonished that even as an adult, he could discover something so utterly new and previously unimagined. It was a revelation to find himself in this living, pulsing world of captivating beauty, life, and mystery, surrounded by the magical colors of the coral, with fish peering curiously or nibbling his fingers. It was meaningful and significant in a way he almost couldn't express. The immediacy and the immersion in something so amazing totally took his breath away.

As he spoke, I realized that this exactly describes what the inner adventure of diamond inquiry (or, simply, inquiry) has been for me. I had been trying for years to describe to people the magnificent world of inquiry and the Diamond Approach. Usually when I'm asked what I do, I say sexy words like "spirituality" and "psychology" and "personal development" and I watch the shutters come down behind most people's eyes. Not always, but mostly. A polite smile and on to the next topic. Or I backpedal to

"Well, I used to be in finance!" to establish some sort of credibility. At least people know what that is.

But really, inquiry is just like scuba diving in the ocean of your inner world. It is as utterly thrilling as lowering yourself into a coral reef or an underwater cave to discover something that you could never have imagined until you encountered it. It is every bit as surprising, magnificent, and unexpected as any ocean diving trip could be, if you know how to enter this world and discover its secrets. One reason you might want to inquire is to discover the richness and wonder of your inner world.

DIVING FOR HIDDEN TREASURES

The inner world is not only an exciting adventure. It is even more personally meaningful than that. The secret depths of the inner world are the very things that we spend our lives longing for: love, wonder, connection, support, belonging, value, meaning, kindness, passion, joy, freedom, determination, power, peace, space. Somewhere between the surface and those magical depths we find the trenches where those things seem to be missing: experiences of being unloved, unsupported, not belonging; of feeling worthless, meaningless, and so on. We manage the circumstances of our ordinary lives above the ocean, sometimes tying ourselves up in knots, to get as much of these qualities as we can and to avoid the trenches. We are heavily influenced by the beliefs and conditioning we grew up with about what these things are and how to get them or even if we can get them. It might never occur to us that the true source of all of these qualities is our very nature, hidden in the depths of our own inner world.

Diamond inquiry takes you diving into your ordinary experience to discover and understand how these hidden qualities are at play, and eventually to discover the inner truth of them in an immediate and palpable way. Little by little as you discover more, your life can become the expression of these qualities from within, rather than the innocent misunderstanding of trying to get them from outside. So that is a second reason you might want to inquire—to discover the truth about these inner treasures beyond what might seem like trenches, with a deeply liberating effect on your life.

Inquiry does not aim for one particular state such as compassion, openness, love, or joy—no matter how wonderful those states are. Instead, inquiry opens you to the possibility of finding whatever it is that is most needed for your particular, personal next step. For example, one time you might need love, but at another time love might not do it—you really need your strength! Sometimes in your life you will need to feel and know your value, while at other times what you most need is to feel some space. Magically, you do not need to know and you do not need to decide—indeed you cannot! But by following and exploring in the way you will learn here, you will be led by the inquiry to exactly what is needed. It is just how the inner world works. In time, you will discover all sorts of different qualities that you might never have imagined.

A PRACTICE FOR CONTEMPORARY LIFE

Diamond inquiry is a practice for contemporary life. We do not live in monasteries. We live rich and full existences with spiritual lives, family lives, love lives, bodily health, sex lives, work lives, financial lives, political lives, community lives, interests, and so on. With inquiry, you can approach and explore experience related to any aspect of life, inner or outer, to find out its deeper truth, to see how it connects with your inner depths. As you do this, you clarify and transform where you are coming from within yourself in meeting that area of life. In this way, inquiry can touch and transform every part of life with a unique, personal directness and immediacy. It brings more truth, exposes the barriers to your inner depths in each situation, and in time allows more realness and freedom, helping you find exactly what you need. And it all happens right in the midst of life, not by leaving life. This makes it uniquely relevant and effective for people today, whether they would think of themselves as spiritual in any traditional sense of the word or not.

INQUIRY AND THE DIAMOND APPROACH

This form of inquiry was discovered and developed by A. H. Almaas, the originator of the Diamond Approach, with his co-originator Karen Johnson and the community of the Ridhwan School that has grown and come to life from their beginnings. The Diamond Approach is an approach to personal development that uses diamond inquiry as the central practice for growth and transformation. The Diamond Approach has given rise to a vast and detailed knowledge of the inner world, and A. H. Almaas has written many books about its nature, dimensions, and hidden treasures. This book focuses on the fundamentals of the practice, since the practice is the key to the entire Diamond Approach teaching. Once you begin to get a sense of *how* to explore here, then you might be interested to read about these various details in more depth since you will have some practical sense of how to explore them directly. Engaging the broader Diamond Approach path through the Ridhwan School with the support of a teacher and a group adds in-depth experiential teaching on particular aspects of the inner ocean. It is like hands-on learning about cave diving, night diving, or reef diving, or going on expeditions to study different marine ecosystems and hidden ocean treasures up close. Of course, the practice of inquiry offers many benefits just on its own, whether or not you choose to learn more about the Diamond Approach.

A BEGINNER'S GUIDE TO A UNIQUE PRACTICE

This book is a hands-on guide to the practice of inquiry. It starts from the very beginning to help you learn how to engage this practice in a way that has been found to work. The method applies whether this is your first step into the inner world or you have many years engaging some spiritual, psychological, embodiment, or other inner practice. So although it is a beginner's book in relation to learning this particular method, that does not mean it is only suitable for people who are just beginning on an inner journey. It can be useful wherever you are in your journey. That being said, you do not need to have any prior experience with inquiry, the Diamond Approach, or any other practice, such as meditation. You do not need to consider yourself spiritual at all. You just need an openness and curiosity to explore yourself and your experience, to discover what is true for you. Also, much of what is here may even be useful if you have been practicing inquiry in the Diamond Approach for a while. A lot of it evolved from my experience of working with students who were either new to the approach or who had been engaging it for several years. It may help you sharpen and round out your practice.

Whatever your experience with the inner world, I invite you to approach diamond inquiry in as open-minded a way as you can, not assuming it to be the same as what you know. There are other practices called inquiry, from other traditions or approaches, and you may find that diamond inquiry shares certain elements with your practice. But it is nonetheless quite distinct, and it may take some time to really "get" the particularity of this practice. The more you discover it, the more you may appreciate its uniqueness.

This book does not require you to believe anything. The same is always true of the practice of inquiry, and indeed of the Diamond Approach more broadly. All it requires is a willingness to look into your own experience in the way you will learn here and to see what you find to be true for yourself.

NAVIGATING THIS BOOK

Each chapter introduces a particular facet of the practice, with at least one exercise, other than in chapter 2, where we deal with practicalities. The exercises allow you to try things out and explore for yourself, which is of utmost importance. Reading about inquiry is not doing it, any more than reading about scuba diving is doing it! So more than anything, I want to encourage you to try it out for yourself!

The book is arranged in three parts. If you were doing a scuba diving course, you would typically start in the pool learning the basics, rather than in the sea. Part one is like this, starting off with some important preparations. You will learn the practicalities of inquiry, which is the equivalent of familiarizing yourself with the scuba gear. Here you will learn two supporting practices that are used in the Diamond Approach. These are not inquiry per se, but they develop important capacities that are needed for inquiry. Kath meditation cultivates your ability to concentrate, which is like learning to stay steady in the water. Sensing, looking, and listening help you get more in touch with your immediate experience in an ongoing way, which is like submersing yourself in the water.

In part two, we head out to sea, introducing the fundamentals of the practice of diamond inquiry itself. You will practice diving into the ocean of your inner world and noticing your thoughts, feelings, sensations, and life circumstances, which are like the sea creatures, coral, and seabed of the inner ocean. Then you will learn how to explore using various questions or questioning attitudes. You will also discover the remarkable openness of inquiry and the transformational magic of it.

Part three of the book goes deeper into some of the main dimensions of the terrain that you will encounter, in the form of the mind, heart, and sensations, and it gives some tips and guidance for exploring these realms. The last chapter is among the most important, so keep going right to the end! A summary brings it all together and may be a helpful prompt when you find yourself splashing around and feeling a bit lost.

Finally, a resources section will point you to various books, websites, and online learning opportunities to support the deepening of your practice and ongoing journey.

PART ONE

At the Pool—
Preparations for
Diamond Inquiry

ONE

What Is the Inner Ocean?

The inner world is in some ways just like the ocean: an entire world beneath the surface of everyday living. From the seashore of ordinary life you might see only a few shells washed up on the beach, some disturbance in the water, or the occasional fish jumping out. But these only hint at the magical world that lies beneath, filled with extraordinary life and hidden treasures. Inquiry means diving in to explore the wonders and riches up close. This is a living world teeming with your thoughts and beliefs, your memories and associations, your feelings and urges, your sensations and impulses, and your very consciousness and beingness itself.

The deeper secrets of the inner ocean are known to very few. Most people might have some idea about fish and coral in the sea. But far fewer know where and how to go diving for pearls, or for hidden jewels and treasures. Similarly, most people have some idea about their thoughts and emotions and the sensations of their bodies, even if they are not deeply in touch with them on a day-to-day basis. But fewer people know of the deeper possibilities beyond a glimpse, much less how to talk about them.

Maybe there is the odd moment when there is a profound feeling of peace, or of connectedness with all of the world. Perhaps there is a deep recognition of the goodness of life or a feeling of joy at the wonder of life. These tiny glimpses sometimes slip by barely noticed, and sometimes they have a very deep impact, possibly changing a life forever. Yet for some reason we seldom consider that these hidden treasures of the inner world are there, accessible in everyday life, to be explored and discovered. There are very few places or social situations in which one would discuss them, and we often do not even have the words to talk about them! We can hardly imagine that they could come into our daily lives and transform them. Yet diamond inquiry is one way for this to happen.

Inquiry is an adventure of discovery. You jump in and look around, to see what there is to see. Something catches your interest and you follow it, wondering what it is, what it is doing there, where it is taking you, what it is about. When you go diving in the sea, there is no fixed formula, no single way to explore underwater caves, to discover the secrets of seahorses, or to restore a coral reef to life. It is up to your curiosity, interest, and skill to guide you. You find yourself in the territory and then navigate according to what is going on right there. Diamond inquiry is the same. In this kind of inquiry, there is no set formula. There are no fixed questions to ask, no set rules to follow, as there are in some other inquiry practices. Here, it is your own living curiosity encountering the immediate reality of your inner world. You are exploring live, right there, as it is happening.

There are, however, some underlying principles and skills, and in this book you will learn some of these principles. When you inquire, you have the freedom to explore your inner world to see and understand whatever comes up. The aim is simply to get as clear as you can about your experience, never assuming that you have discovered all there is to discover, being curious to understand yourself and your experience. This clarity can be like the exquisite clarity of a diamond, which is where the name comes from.

As the name *inquiry* implies, the practice fundamentally involves asking questions. More accurately, it involves approaching your experience with an inquiring and curious attitude. It is not about questions with right or wrong answers but rather open questions that express your interest. Just like when you dive underwater and wonder, "Oh, what's here?" Then you spot something and think, "Hmm, I wonder what that is?" The questioning expresses a gently curious, open, contemplating attitude toward what you are finding in your inner world. We will get more into this later, but for now, you might take a moment and see if you can get a feeling of taking that orientation toward yourself. How would it feel to be open and curious toward yourself?

THE INNER OCEAN

Before we start learning to dive, let us first get some orientation to the inner ocean. What is it exactly that we will be exploring? The inner world of a human being is extraordinarily rich and complex. The human brain is the most complex structure we know in the universe, capable of allowing us to live and experience all the facets of life that we do. Here are some of the possibilities of the inner world. With each one I mention, or with those that seem to catch your attention, feel free to take a few moments to see if you can recognize that element in your own experience. There might be some you recognize from times in the past. There might also be some elements arising right here in the present moment as you are contemplating, so you can look at them live, in the moment as they are happening. There might also be some possibilities I mention that you do not recognize at all, and that is completely fine too—let your curiosity be piqued!

- Your inner ocean pulses with the sensations of all different parts of your body from your toes to the top of your head. It is alive with your sense perceptions of seeing, hearing, tasting, smelling, and touching the world around you and the world inside you.
- It can throb with instinctual drives for security, social connection, or sexual connection. Consider how you might feel if you suddenly gained a large amount of money that made you more secure—or if you suddenly lost your money or your job!
- Your inner life is lit up by your mind. Here, *mind* means the conventional sense of your thoughts, the flow of your inner dialogue, the images of your imagination and memory, and the beliefs that shape and structure your experience and help you make sense of it. *Mind* can also refer to your very capacities of awareness and consciousness themselves—the direct knowing of what is happening in your experience as it is happening. These capacities enable you to recognize and know in the immediacy of the moment that that is a chair and that is a dog. You see the chair and you just know that it is a chair—the knowing happens right there. It is the same when you recognize that you are feeling happy, when you are. Your mind has this basic ability to tell one thing from another, to recognize experiences for what they

are, and to build up memories and ideas about things. Your mind also has the potential for understanding. *Mind* can be used in the Buddhist sense, referring to the whole of the inner ocean, but we will not be using it in that sense here.

• Your inner life is colored and animated by your feelings and emotions. These can range from emotional reactions such as anger, sadness, fear, or boredom to more positive feelings such as happiness, love, or contentment.

• Your inner ocean is made of the pure qualities of your human nature. These are qualities such as intelligence, love, groundedness, kindness, joy, passion, or openness, to name a few. We call these your nature, your essence, your spirit. These inner qualities come built in with every human being; they are the hidden treasures of the inner ocean. Everyone has them to some extent; they are active in everybody. But most people do not recognize them directly. You may or may not have thought of these qualities as "spiritual," but really all I mean is that they are the intrinsic, inherent qualities of your nature. We will see as we go diving that these qualities can appear as qualities of *presence*, as the very immediate hereness of your consciousness. You will learn that it is possible to directly sense and know the presence of your own beingness, with all these different qualities. The way these qualities are lived and expressed in your life is shaped by the next item—your conditioning.

• The inner world and your essential nature are shaped by all the memories, impressions, learnings, and associations that have come from your personal history. Your learning stretches back from something you experienced a moment ago, or learned yesterday, all the way back to your childhood and your earliest life. This vast learning we call your *conditioning*. It is your "nurture" in the sense that it is learned, in contrast to your nature, which is intrinsic. Many of the details of your learning and conditioning had to be acquired; they do not all come built in. Your conditioning includes your psychology—the specific influences of your early life on the way that your nature is expressed through your personality.

- Your inner life and your conditioning include particular judgments that you should be this way or that way and should not be other ways. This appears in the way you sometimes beat yourself up or give yourself a hard time about how you are doing or what you are experiencing.

- Your inner life is centered around your sense of yourself, your identity. Who and what you experience yourself to be has many levels and is continually changing. It includes everything that you experience as "me" at different times, including ideas in your mind or familiar feelings that you have, your sense of self based on your history or the immediacy of your presence. There are even ways of experiencing your identity as a boundless infinite presence, as no sense of self at all.

- Your inner world includes the way you feel and experience other people and all the aspects of your circumstances and the world around you—everything that you might experience as "not me." It includes the way you experience the connection or relationship between what is you and what is around you.

- Your inner ocean includes your completely ordinary day-to-day sense of consciousness.

- Your inner world encompasses all of what you might call positive experiences and negative experiences.
- Your inner ocean is your own particular individual experience, which is different from that of the person next to you. They have their own experience of reality that might—or might not!—be the same as or similar to yours in any given moment. This is sometimes called the "first-person givenness" of experience, the fact that your experience is *your* experience. It is true even in the more exotic spiritual experiences—for example, when you experience the person next to you being one with you or of the same nature as you. After all, they themselves might not be experiencing that even though you experience it as being true!
- Your inner ocean is continually ebbing and flowing, changing and transforming, growing and unfolding throughout your life. There is quite literally an infinite potential of experience. Life can be a journey of learning, development, and emergence without end.

All these elements are like a living underwater ecosystem where everything is interconnected and dependent on everything else. In the sea, the fish, shells, seaweed, and coral are all linked with one another and with the water conditions, temperature, rock formations, and nearby cities. Similarly, your feelings and beliefs, your history and the personal details of what you love or enjoy, and the very qualities of your human nature itself are all intimately and meaningfully connected in the ecosystem of your inner life.

In diamond inquiry, you directly explore your conscious experience in a way that unlocks these potentials. You consciously enter into the very palpable sense of your experience and explore it just like a diver exploring a reef. You will discover wondrous treasures, terrifying monsters, deep trenches, infinite expanses, and limitless potential and freedom. You will find the snarled-up discarded fishing nets from years ago that are keeping the inner life-forms trapped within you. As you explore and understand what you find, it transforms and some new potential that was hidden within the garbage emerges with unforeseen beauty.

Best of all, in a way that even real ocean scuba diving cannot match, these discoveries are *you*—they are the very nature of who and what you actually are. The inner world is invisible to the ordinary eye at first. But as you learn how to see and touch this world, the adventure becomes even more immersive than the highest definition or most vivid 3D television or movie. You are not exploring something outside of yourself; in diamond inquiry you are exploring your very consciousness itself. It is intimate, immediate, personal, meaningful, and relevant. It brings you to that which feels most meaningful and central in any given aspect of your life.

And just like diving in the outer ocean, at the beginning it takes a certain amount of time in the proverbial pool to get used to the gear and to learn how to orient yourself and get about. You need to find your way around what might seem like a muddy little resort pond for a bit, before you clear the outlet into the swampy bay, and then the magnificent reef beyond, with glistening pearls hidden in the depths.

A. H. Almaas, one of the originators of the Diamond Approach, likens inquiry to a space cruiser in his book *Spacecruiser Inquiry*. The practice is a vehicle of inner travel through which you explore different inner experiential worlds, galaxies, and even universes. So perhaps diving and exploring the seas on *this* world is a good analogy for the first step toward exploring other planets. This book is intended to help you get started. It is a guide to entering the shallows of the inner world. If this whets your appetite for inner exploration and adventures, then when you have your bearings in the earthly seas, the distant planets and galaxies will be waiting.

EXERCISE: PEEKING BELOW

Now, having touched on some of the possibilities, you are going to take your first step toward an inquiry exercise. For this informal exploration, you can just sit comfortably in a quiet spot. This will take about five to ten minutes. You can keep a notebook or journal next to you if you like. As you do this exercise, you can speak your observations out loud or jot down notes on paper.

In this first exercise, you will simply take some time to be aware of the elements appearing in the flow of your inner world right now in what we call a *continuum of awareness*. You are going to dip your head into the water and look around to see how the water is, what sort of seabed you are over, what fish are swimming nearby—by this, I mean whatever arises in your awareness as you are doing this practice. What kind of feelings are around? What is on your mind? What sensations are you in touch with? See if you are in touch, as you are looking, with any of the elements that were just mentioned. You do not need to try to hold on to that list or remember it, or to be limited by it. Just peek at your immediate awareness now and see what you find arising in your experience this moment. Inquiry is always about the direct immediacy of your experience, and this is the first moment in this book to check that out directly.

Take your time as you are doing this exercise, as if you are totally at leisure. There is no pressure, no rush, no specific thing you are supposed to find, so you cannot get it wrong. See if you can take the attitude of "Hmm . . . what's here? What's going on inside me? What am I noticing?" Contemplate your inner world with open interest.

To assist your inquiry, speak your observations out loud, or use a journal to write a sentence or phrase about what you notice. Then take a moment and pause. And then see what is happening in the next moment. You simply keep repeating this moment by moment, looking in to see what is there and noting whatever it happens to be.

The exercise might go something like this, with a comfortable few-seconds pause between each awareness: "I'm experiencing a feeling of curiosity . . . I feel a slight apprehension . . . there's an ache in my hip . . . I feel excited about my date tonight . . . I have an urge to get up, I'm not sure I want to carry on with this . . . I wonder if I'm doing this right . . . hmm . . . not much . . . still not much . . . I see the view out the windows . . . I feel a sense of stillness . . . the stillness feels like a deep vastness . . ." and so on.

Stay with the flow of your inner experience without particularly trying to do anything to it or make anything happen. If you do find yourself trying to do something or make something happen, then you could simply notice that as what is arising. You might say, "Oh, now I'm trying to find something to say," or "Now I'm trying to make myself feel good in some way." If you find yourself judging what you are experiencing, you might just notice and mention that. So the exercise is simply to notice whatever it might be that appears in your awareness moment by moment. It is as inwardly focused as meditation, but it is more active than meditation, in that you are noting out loud or in writing whatever you find happening in your awareness in that moment.

Do this for five or ten minutes. You can use a timer to keep time for you and tell you when to stop.

Afterward, take a breath, in through your nose and out through your mouth. Part of the magic of the inner world is that the very act of getting in touch can begin to change things. So notice how it has affected you to peer into your inner world in this way. Say or write a few sentences about that.

Between now and when you read the next chapter, take some time—perhaps five or ten minutes, a couple of times a day—to dip your head into your inner world and notice what is arising in your consciousness. Be as open and curious as you can be to see whatever shows up from the whole range of inner experience. You are hanging out with this question: "Hmm . . . what's here . . . what am I experiencing?" You could try this at different times—perhaps when you wake up; after a meditation or yoga session, if you do that; after a workout; after a day at work; or after hanging out with a friend. Different situations will tend to bring up different elements in your inner world. And after you have peered around, take a minute to notice how it has affected you to do so.

TWO

The Practical Diving Gear of Inquiry

Before you actually hit the water to go diving, you need some tools and skills—some swimwear, perhaps a mask, the ability to swim, and some understanding of where you are going. It is the same with diamond inquiry. So let us begin with some of the basics about how, when, and where to inquire.

WHERE AND WHEN TO INQUIRE

It is good to make time for a regular, formal inquiry practice when you are least likely to be disturbed, when there are not too many other things pulling on your attention. Developing the skill of inquiry is just like learning any other skill: it takes time and regular practice. Without regular practice, you simply cannot learn to inquire, any more than you could learn to go diving in the sea without practicing that.

Fifteen to twenty minutes is a good practice period. If something captures your interest during your practice, there is no reason not to inquire for longer if you like. But even in that case, take a break after fifteen to twenty minutes. Have a walk, sit quietly, or do a short meditation for a few minutes before going into another period of inquiry. This will help your inquiry to land. While it may seem that "more is better," in fact it is best to let your system absorb and digest what you have found, rather than continuing to take in more and more.

For formal practice, find a place that is quiet, relatively free from distraction, and private, so that you need not be concerned about being overheard. Ideally, you want to be able to say and express whatever you want during your inquiry—this will give you maximum freedom. That said, if for some reason the only place available is somewhere with others nearby, then you can always do a silent written inquiry, with less outward expression.

There is no set posture or position for inquiry. You can do it sitting at your desk or a table or on the sofa, speaking out loud or writing in your notebook or on a computer. You could even be standing up or lying down. In time, as you get more practiced, you could go for an inquiry walk.

While the particular position is not so important as such, there are a few things to be aware of. It is important to stay awake, attentive and tuned in to your inner experience. If you easily fall asleep when you lie down or sit on a very comfortable sofa, then those will probably not be good positions for you to inquire. Conversely, if you are uncomfortable sitting in a particular chair or if you get tired standing, then your attention may be dominated by your discomfort rather than your inquiry, so then those are not good positions for you.

You want to be able to sense as much of your body as you can, and you will learn to sense more fully and finely into your sensations in this book. It is therefore helpful to have your body be unrestricted. Meditation postures, such as the lotus position, that restrict your legs (or some other body part) are therefore not suggested, and nor is very tight or uncomfortably restrictive clothing.

There is no need to sit rigidly or maintain a fixed posture while you inquire, so let your body be alive and part of your exploration. There may be times in your inquiry when you want to get really expressive—for example, when exploring a very energetic state such as excitement or anger. In this case—whether sitting, lying down, or standing up—it is helpful to be able to move around in a way that allows you to continue exploring and discovering your inner experience. In a couple of the exercises in this book, you will need two chairs facing each other to represent two parts of your inner world, and that is also a setup that is useful at times.

INQUIRY ON YOUR OWN

Inquiry is easily practiced on your own. It is important to develop the capacity to inquire into your experience yourself, so that you are not dependent on always having inquiry partners or a teacher, however helpful they may be.

Monologue Inquiry

The most common way to inquire is to do a monologue, which involves talking out loud. Here, you are speaking out your inquiry, exploring your experience and talking about it as you do so. There are many benefits to doing your inquiry out loud. Speaking and hearing yourself often has a tangibly different impact than simply relying on thought.

Written Inquiry

You can also do your inquiry in written form on your computer or in your journal. Some people like to write things out in full, and others prefer to simply jot down key points as they explore without writing out full sentences. This is up to you. At the beginning, it is probably better to err on the side of writing more than less. As you become more proficient, you may be able to track your process and explore it without writing down every word.

Silent Inquiry

In time, you will be able to inquire silently by yourself—for example, just sitting or walking and contemplating your experience. You will be able to inquire "on the fly" when something interesting comes up, even while you are doing something else. That said, even after decades, there is often an extra level of clarity and definiteness that comes with the discipline of formally doing it out loud or in writing, so this is always recommended as the backbone of your practice.

INQUIRY WITH SILENT WITNESSES

Other people can be tremendous support for inquiry. You can meet and inquire in person together, or you can use Skype, Face-Time, Zoom, or the like to meet virtually and inquire. You can inquire with one other person or with a couple of other people.

Inquiring with a silent witness is like going diving in your inner world with a diving buddy. Your buddy completely lets you lead the dive, going wherever you want to go and exploring whatever you want to explore while simply staying present with you. They are not there to tell you what to do or where to go, or whether your inner ocean is right or not! They are just there to witness and accompany you while you dive.

The suggested approach when working with one or more partners is for each person to do a monologue. Agree to a time—such as ten or fifteen minutes—and then let each person have that period of time to do their own monologue inquiry while the others are silent witnesses. When one person finishes, there can be a short pause to reset the timer and then the next person begins. Go around until you have all had your turn.

Being the Inquirer

Do your inquiry out loud, verbalizing and exploring your experience in a monologue. Just sitting in silence for an extended time is not inquiry, although you might take some time to sit and contemplate in silence as you begin or at various points throughout the inquiry. But at some point, you need to say something about what is happening. The next chapters will explore the actual inquiry process itself.

When you are inquiring with witnesses, you are not doing it for their benefit or entertainment. You do not need to try to explain yourself to them or make sure that they understand you or your experience. You are not telling them a story. Your exploration is really just for you. It is for your own recognition and understanding of yourself and your experience. It is purely for your own benefit to discover a bit more of what is true for you. The witnesses are just there to support you in doing your own exploration.

Being the Silent Witness

As the witness, your job is to remain as neutral, present, and open as you can. In chapter 5, you will learn a practice called *sensing*, *looking*, and *listening*; as the witness, all you need to do is to sense, look, and listen and remain connected with whatever is going on inside you while attending to the other person. The more you sense yourself, the more you will naturally feel how the other person's inquiry might be affecting you. For example, you might be touched by what they say; you might feel happy, or judgmental, or like you want to give them advice. It is part of the practice to allow and feel whatever it is that happens inside you as you witness them, but not to overtly express any of it. You stay outwardly silent and neutral. You give the person doing the monologue the space to see and experience whatever they do, however they do, without overtly influencing them. You do not need to make them feel better, therapize, fix, coach, advise, nudge, encourage, or discourage them in any way. Your presence and openness is the greatest gift you can give here. It really does make a difference, even though you might think at first that you are not doing much.

Being the silent witness or receiving this kind of spacious and nonreactive witnessing can feel a little unfamiliar at first. It is not a common way of being with someone in daily life, especially if you are more used to advising or helping other people. In time, you will very likely come to recognize that it offers great freedom, respect, and trust.

When inquiring together with someone new, I recommend using this basic type of silent witnessing for a couple of months. Allow yourselves to get used to giving and receiving the openness and noninterference. It is important to appreciate silent witnessing's value before you become more active, as I will describe next, no matter how tempting it might seem.

INQUIRY WITH AN ACTIVE WITNESS

If you and your inquiry companion(s) have had some experience of doing inquiry and are comfortable inquiring with each other and with open, nonexpressive witnessing, then you might add a further step. After one person's monologue period, take a further five minutes to continue the inquiry, during which the witnesses can offer some questions to help the inquirer see and understand a bit more about their experience. So each person will get, say, fifteen minutes of monologue and then a further five minutes of ongoing inquiry with questions from the witnesses.

Inquiring with an active witness is also like having a diving buddy along with you, but now they are doing a bit more. At the end of your dive, your buddy might ask you about something that they noticed on the dive, and you might swim back to check it out and discover something new. It can be very helpful to have another curious and friendly pair of eyes accompanying you, perhaps to notice something you did not or simply to be interested in your inner world with you.

What might the witness or witnesses ask? As a witness, you might have noticed something in the inquiry that you did not quite understand, or a particular moment where you were not sure what the inquirer was feeling or what was going on. So you might ask them a question about that. You might have gotten curious about something they said, and then invite them to say more about that. Or they might have seemed to skip over something that drew your attention and you might ask them what was going on there. We will be exploring many different types of questions throughout this book, and you might find one angle that the person did not explore so much but that made you curious—and then ask them about that.

As with being a silent witness, the active witness's intention is not to advise, fix, or change anything, nor is it to get a person to see the brilliant insight you might have had about them. The idea is to ask open questions, to open the possibility for the inquirer to explore and understand more for themselves about their own process and experience. The questions come out of the same open and noninterfering stance of the silent witness. You are simply sharing a question that occurred to you or a curiosity that you had while you were witnessing them. You offer them a possibility of getting clearer about their experience.

If you are receiving the questions from your witnesses, feel free to take the time to consider the invitation of each question, to see if you want to respond to it and explore further. Remember that the intention of any question in inquiry is not to come up with a right or wrong answer. The question is an invitation to swim a little closer to something and check it out a bit more to see what else you might see. You are always free not to respond, or to leave a question aside if it does not feel right to you or if it feels like it is asking too much.

INQUIRY WITH A BOOK

Inquiry can also be used as a practice to support your understanding of any spiritual or contemplative book you might be reading. As mentioned earlier, many books have been written on different elements of the inner world. The books by A. H. Almaas are particularly relevant because they describe the way the inner world is discovered and unfolds through this particular practice. Other books may be helpful too.

You can relate to a book purely as intellectual information to take in mentally and think about, and that has a certain utility, but this is not the most practical and transformational use of it. A more practical approach is to treat the book as a boat that takes you out in the direction of a particular aspect of your inner world and then starts shining a few flashlights down into the water to give you hints for what to look out for. Bear in mind that this does not mean that you will immediately start finding what the book has been telling you about, just as you are not guaranteed to find dolphins if you take the boat out to a spot where dolphins are known to surface. The book is more an invitation to be open to certain possibilities that might show up.

If you'd like to use inquiry to more deeply explore a book you are reading, prepare first with a session of meditation and sensing, looking, and listening (as you will learn later in this book). Then read a section or chapter of the book slowly or even out loud, letting yourself take in and be affected by what you are reading. After you have a read a bit, stop and then do an inquiry to explore as you will learn to do here. In other words, let yourself be where you are and explore whatever the reading is bringing up for you in your immediate experience, whatever is nudging into awareness in your inner world. It might be what you are reading about or something else altogether. You can trust that whatever is coming up is the most important thing for you to explore, even if it seems to have nothing to do with what you were reading. If it is an advanced book, it may be pointing to something quite far down in the depths, and you may have to do a lot of inquiry and clarifying in the shallows before your inner ocean can reveal the depths you have been reading about. This is not a bad thing or a problem. It is just naturally how the inner world works!

INQUIRY WITH A TEACHER

Inquiry with a teacher is a further possibility. A Diamond Approach teacher is like a master diver who has vast experience exploring their own inner world as well as the skill and capacity to guide another in their exploration.

Going on retreat with a teacher is like going out on a diving trip to see and explore a particular island or reef. Teachers can also work one-on-one with you as you go exploring in your inner world. In your own explorations, the chances are good that sooner or later you will come to something that you do not know how to deal with, something you cannot seem to solve or understand, some way in which you seem to get stuck. The teacher can explore it with you and help you find your way.

They might point out to you something in your experience that you had not noticed or thought to explore. You may swim past a little opening in the reef a hundred times until someone who knows what kind of creatures lurk in that exact kind of opening says, "Hey, just hang out by that opening for a while and let's see what happens!" Sometimes the most interesting doorways in our experience are those that we ourselves would simply skim past unless someone else helped us to see them. Or you might not want to explore some particular experience by yourself because it feels unfamiliar or unsafe. A teacher can be very helpful in all these situations.

A teacher can help you not only navigate particular territory but also learn to inquire more skillfully. They can show you how to enter the caves, or discover the treasure hidden inside some seemingly impenetrable clam, or learn how to swim safely with dolphins or great white sharks! Even more than that, a Diamond Approach teacher knows about the hidden secrets, the jewels of the inner ocean that are beyond the normal seascapes and creatures. They can help you dive in a way that will open up these magical possibilities in yourself. At times, the teacher's inner ocean may even resonate with your own inner world, opening up further possibilities in you.

If inquiry turns out to be something you get turned on to, and a teacher is available to you, it may well be worth exploring some sessions. The resources section at the end of the book can help you locate a teacher, if you decide you would like to work with one.

THREE

Seeing Underwater with the Mask of Friendly Interest

If you have taken some time to dip your head into the water and see what is around using the exercise in chapter 1, you have probably noticed that there are some experiences that you like and are happy to see and to be in touch with. Many people like it when they feel on top of things, or kind and loving, or open, or content. It is all good when they are able to think happy thoughts about themselves or their lives, or when their body or energy is feeling good and healthy. But becoming more aware of your inner experience might also reveal some less comfortable things. You might wonder why you would want to get in touch with those.

For example, you might think that anger is bad. Maybe you wish you weren't so nervous at work or that you were more loving and spiritual. Maybe you wish you could break this or that habit, or not feel sad about some particular situation. You might want to get rid of those critical thoughts that come up every time you see your friend. If you have done some spiritual work, you might have decided you want to be free from your ego, or to let go of your mind and its busyness, or to move into acceptance (and paradoxically away from whatever it is that you are experiencing). You might encounter various discomforts, tensions, or even illness in your body. These are examples of elements arising within your inner ocean that you might find yourself wanting to reject, change, move away from, or at any rate not experience fully.

As you begin to look, you will probably see all kinds of preferences, attitudes, and even judgments about what you encounter in your experience. You might notice that you try to avoid certain feelings, perceptions, or thoughts. You might see yourself trying to change yourself, your life, or those around you, so that you do not have to experience certain elements that come up in your inner world. Or you might be on a self-improvement path, determined to be the very best you and only think positive thoughts.

All of this is quite understandable. Of course it makes sense that you want to be happy or free; to feel better or to be more fully yourself; to have a positive experience and not a negative experience. If you have discovered some of your deeper potentials such as love, strength, or value, it would naturally make sense that you want to experience them more. Emotional reactions such as anger, sadness, or frustration seem less desirable, or they seem to get in the way of what you want.

But there is a fundamental difficulty with this. Trying to change, fix, or improve your experience is basically rejecting yourself and what is going on inside you, and that seldom makes you feel better. Think about it for a moment. Suppose you are sitting with a friend, and your friend is upset. What would be more helpful? Would it help things if you yelled at your friend and told her to get over it? Would it help if you pushed her away and told her you only want to see her when she is in a good mood? How would that make her feel? Probably not great. She might put on a brave face for a bit, but sooner or later that upset would probably come back, and either she would have to hide it from you next time or pretend it wasn't there, which would mean being fake with you. None of that would deepen your friendship!

In contrast, imagine how it would be if you said to her, "Oh wow, you seem really upset! What's going on? Tell me what's happened!" How would it be to have a friendly, interested attitude to find out what is upsetting her and to be with her just as she is?

Then your friend might tell you something about what has upset her, and as you talk it through with her, she might begin to calm down as she gets some perspective. Maybe somebody criticized her work in a mean way and she felt hurt and put down. And what she really needs is some kindness to acknowledge the hurt and help her move through it. After a few moments, she might look back at what happened and see that what the person said was untrue. She would get clearer about what had happened and start coming back to life. She might realize she does not need to take that kind of criticism from anyone; she can take input, but not being attacked. Suddenly she might find herself feeling clear and confident about that. So through this conversation in response to your friendly interest, she would see a bit more clearly what is actually true. She would find some strength to deal with these kinds of circumstances next time, some more kindness for when things are hard, and some more resilience to come through the experience. Her experience would have deepened and opened up as you let her be with her truth and find out more about it. If you had just pushed her away and told her to get over it and get on with it, she might not have gotten there.

This is the kind of friendly interest you bring to your experience when you inquire. You try to be kind and curious about yourself and your situation. This will help you to be with the situation and explore to understand what is happening within you in a transformational way. This attitude is not the only thing that is needed, but without it, it is hard to even start.

This does not apply only to difficult experiences. What if your friend is madly in love? You could bring an attitude like, "Don't be ridiculous, love is for fools!" or "Oh, remember what happened last time you fell in love?" Or you might feel jealous and not want to know about her love. These are all attitudes that are not friendly and interested and will probably close down your friend's love, or at any rate make her not want to share her experience and her truth with you. In contrast, how would it be to be kind and curious? "Oh wow, you're in love! Tell me about it! Who are you in love with? What do you love about them? How does it feel to be in love?" This kind of attitude will invite your friend to land in her love and discover more about it.

If you are honest about it, isn't this what you would like? Wouldn't it be great if you could just be where you are, with whatever is going on for you, good or bad, and be able to be honest and truthful about it? And perhaps curious and interested too? For many of us, this kind of friendly interest in our own experience is surprisingly rare and quite unexpected. More often, we are prone to interfere with our experience—to reject it, judge it, or try to fix it.

So contemplate this for a moment. What if nothing is wrong or broken? What if nothing that happens within you is a mistake? What if you do not have to change yourself? What if you can simply be kind and interested in what is happening within you? What if you could be that kind of friend for yourself? You do not have to like it if it is not comfortable. You do not have to get rid of your preferences. You actually do not have to get rid of anything. But could you be friendly enough with yourself to take an interest in where you actually are, to be open to yourself and curious to understand what it is about, whether it is fantastic, just OK, or downright awful? Could you be interested in exploring whatever corner of the inner ocean you happen to be finding yourself in?

This quality of friendly, kind curiosity and interest is an inherent and natural quality of a human being. It is one of the buried jewels of the inner ocean. Our friendly interest is covered over by all our history and conditioning, where our own need for friendliness was not met. We learned that our experience was not welcome, when people in our lives—and particularly our early family life—did not welcome us with curiosity and care, wherever we happened to be.

In its place, we tend to have a range of rejecting attitudes toward our experience for a variety of reasons. We tend not to be friendly and interested in experiences that are difficult, painful, or negative in some way. We tend not to be kind and curious about experiences that feel empty, where something that we like seems missing, or that seem familiar or boring in some way. We might not be friendly and curious about experiences that are unfamiliar or that we do not understand. We tend not to be kind toward and interested in experiences that we think will have undesirable consequences in our lives. We tend not to be open to experiences that we might have had before, that were not welcomed by other people who are important to us—experiences that we have learned are not to be welcomed, explored, or talked about. It is good to be aware of these possibilities so that when you find yourself not being friendly and interested in something that is arising within you, you can check and see why that is. What is making you reject your experience?

This natural quality has been squashed, put away, or obscured to some degree. In our practice of diamond inquiry, we are finding and practicing that attitude again, as best we can. For sure, you will not always feel friendly and interested toward yourself or your experience! But you can try it out by looking into whatever is happening in your experience and seeing what happens if you do not do the usual thing of pushing your experience away. Instead, try getting curious about yourself and being your own best friend.

Diamond inquiry is open to anything that you experience. It turns out that absolutely everything that arises in your experience is meaningful. The fact that it is there is not an accident but rather reflects something going on in yourself to be allowed, explored, and eventually understood. It might seem surprising to consider that even a difficult experience will eventually lead to something true and real and good. All you need to do is hold it as a possibility and then see for yourself. There will almost certainly be times you doubt that opening to what you are experiencing will turn out well. But in time you might find for yourself how true this is, even if some experience takes a long time to reveal its inner truth and beauty.

The more we practice this friendly interest and see the ways that we block it and the reasons for doing so, the more the waters of our inner ocean begin to transform. Your inner world can begin to feel friendly, inviting, and life-giving. Even when there is a raging shark or dying coral reef in our immediate focus, even when we are upset or afraid, there can be an atmosphere of care and curiosity. The waters of the inner ocean are alive, warm, intimate, friendly; they embrace every inner experience with curiosity in just the right way. We can begin to sense and recognize the very presence of friendly, interested consciousness as who and what we are. If we follow the kind curiosity of our inner world to its very source, we might find it emanating from a shining green jewel of pure friendliness, whose warmth and light can pervade the inner world. We will see more about these inner treasures as we go.

EXERCISE: EXPLORING YOUR ATTITUDE

If you like, you can begin with a bow, a dedication. Bring your hands to your forehead and bow deeply, honoring your inner nature and truth with a friendly, open, and interested attitude toward you and all that you might experience.

Now take some time to explore your attitude toward your inner experience. You want to see and understand some of what limits your friendly attitude toward yourself. You can do this in three parts.

First, take, say, ten minutes to make a list of some experiences that you are not so friendly with. See what elements of your inner world you usually judge or want to change, fix, or get rid of. These might appear as feelings that you do not like to feel. They could be positive or negative—maybe you do not like to feel frustration or failure, emotional pain or discomfort of some kind, or perhaps too much excitement or love. They could be sensations that seem unwelcome to you—maybe you think something is wrong if you feel empty in some way or if you feel some kind of pleasure or tingling. And they could be thoughts or perceptions that you do not like to admit, such as seeing selfishness in your actions or those of a friend. Just roll with it. Let various experiences come to mind that you tend not to welcome and be open to.

After you have made your list, pause and take a moment to notice how it has affected you to do this. How are you feeling in the moment? How is it to look at this list and recognize the elements of your experience that you usually push away? How is your breathing? Take a nice deep breath, filling first your belly and then your chest and then simply letting it out freely through your mouth. And another one.

Then, for the second part, take another ten minutes to explore some of your own reasons for being less than open and friendly with these various experiences. You are going to practice being friendly and interested in what limits your friendly interest! I have mentioned some of the possible reasons earlier, and you might find others. Choose an item on your list and explore for yourself why you are not open and interested in yourself when you are having that experience. Ask yourself in a friendly, interested way, "What is right about not being welcoming of and interested in that experience?" Some part of you must think that there are good reasons not to go there or you would not have this attitude, and you are inviting yourself to see and understand these attitudes and beliefs. You might think the feeling is inappropriate, or negative; perhaps it seems not to be going anywhere, or pointless; or irrelevant. You might have seen other people experience something similar and not want to be like them. So there might be all sorts of reasons. You do not need to think too hard about it. You are just shining a flashlight down into the water to see why this particular kind of fish might not be welcome. Say or jot down the first couple of points that come to mind in response to your friendly interest. Then pause for a moment and move on to another item on your list: "What's right about not being welcoming of *this* experience if it starts coming up?"

At the end of the ten minutes, pause again. Take another couple of breaths, filling your belly and your chest and letting it out freely through your mouth. How has it affected you to get friendly and interested in why you push away your experience? How are you feeling now? Do you understand a little more about yourself? Do you feel more understanding of yourself, as you simply give yourself some space to notice what seems unwelcome and why?

In the last part of the exercise, you will now directly explore what it is like to be with yourself in a friendly and interested way, using a Gestalt technique. We sometimes use this technique to explore the connection between two parts of our inner world.

If you can, take two chairs and arrange them as if there are two close friends that really care about each other sitting and talking together, in whatever way seems most comfortable and friendly to you. Designate one chair to be "you," just as you are. Designate the second chair to be the attitude and feeling of friendly interest.

Begin sitting in "your" chair. As you sit here, just being yourself, imagine a kind, interested person, as if you were sitting with the most warm and friendly person. Allow whatever comes up as you do this. You might feel quite touched by the possibility. You might have no sense of it at all and think it is a silly exercise. You might feel that you do not want them to get too close to you, or it might feel relaxing to be finally sitting with someone who is not trying to change you. Just allow and notice whatever happens and try to stay curious about whatever comes up. Now see if there is something you would like to say to the presence in that other chair—and if there is, go ahead and say it as if you are speaking to someone sitting there.

Then move over to the chair of friendly interest and imagine yourself relating back to "you" in "your" chair in this kind way. Notice how you feel in this position. How is it to imagine looking back at yourself, relating to "you" sitting there, in a friendly way? What would you say to yourself? Take your time to feel this out. If nothing comes up, try starting with a simple "Hi!"

And then continue the conversation, physically moving back over to "your" chair and letting yourself receive the friendly interest coming from the other chair. And see what you want to say back.

Go back and forth between "you" and "friendly interest," letting yourself alternate on the two sides of the conversation for ten minutes. Just be as spontaneous as you can be and let whatever comes come. There is no right or wrong with this exercise!

At the end, take a breath and notice how you are feeling now. Say something about how it has affected you to do this exercise, allowing whatever it is that is stirring in you.

We have been exploring the attitude of inquiry, which is one of friendly interest in whatever arises in you. This is an unusual kind of openness, a deep invitation to let yourself simply be as you are, whether it is sublime or tied up in knots, and to simply be curious about what is going on. Whatever is there in your inner world is there for a reason—there is something personally relevant and important going on there for you, and the most helpful thing you can do is to take an interest in yourself, to open yourself to your experience and in turn to invite your experience to open up and reveal more. This is actually the natural attitude of our beingness, but it may not be obvious at first if there are a lot of agendas in the way. Remember, if you find it takes a long time to discover this attitude, be friendly with yourself about that too. It might not simply spring up overnight!

Before moving to the next chapter, here is a way to continue practicing, to help you see more. Take five to ten minutes to practice at different times of your day. Start off remembering this attitude of friendly interest and then dip into your inner experience and see where you are: What is on your mind? What circumstances are up for you? What are you feeling? How is your energy? Stay in the flow of your experience and see what happens as you do. At the end, take a moment to look back and see if you were able to be open and friendly with whatever was going on. Also notice if you had trouble with that, if you were rejecting your experience or trying to fix or change something. If so, what limited your friendly interest in your experience? How does it seem to affect things when you are more friendly or less friendly?

Question and Answer: Friendly Interest

I just do not feel friendly and interested in myself at all. I do not seem to care about myself or about this experience that I'm having. I certainly do not want to know anything more about it! How can I inquire from here?

This is a very interesting experience to recognize! You might consider letting that be the experience that you are having, and be as friendly and interested in that as you can be: "Oh, wow. Yes, I see I really do not care. I really am totally uninterested in myself." How is it to let that be the truth, to not have to force yourself to care or be interested when you are not? How can you be friendly with that part of your psyche? Being kind and curious means not trying to change it, so that you give it space. But it also means not just getting up and walking away. So you do not go, "OK, well that's it, I'm not interested. So much for scuba diving!" Instead, you stay there. You continue to hang out in this particular place until it begins to open up and reveal more. Chances are there is some history caught up in there, waiting for you to untangle it. In the coming chapters you will learn how to explore into any experience, including that one. We are just at the beginning here, but do not let that—or any other experience—stop you quite so easily.

When I look inside my inner world, I just start to feel anxiety. Surely this is bad for me, and a friend would want me to feel better!

It might be true that your friend would want you not to feel anxious. But the feeling of anxiety is there inside you! So you can either cover it up and pretend it is not there—which will leave it untouched and always waiting to jump out at you—or you could inquire into it to find out what it is, what is making it happen, whether it is real, and so on. Bringing the experience into the light to be felt and understood will help you come to terms with it in a much deeper way than simply trying to get rid of it. The same can be said of any negative experience.

Inquiring into your experience at the beginning often feels a bit like hard work. Our inner experience might have all sorts of difficult feelings, things we are trying not to feel or see about our situation. Our whole personality has developed to keep us away from these things! Inquiry will, little by little, open that all up. The good news is that, in time, we begin clearing out the swamp. Although you have to pinch your nose with your fingers to go into some particularly smelly patch of water, once you get to the bottom of it and unblock the outlet, things will to start flow and your inner ocean will begin to clear up. The path of inquiry goes into these difficult places little by little. By discovering what is going on there, we help them reveal their natural potential. You will see more about this as we go along.

When I do the practice, I find the same old thing coming up over and over. I've been working on this same issue for so many years and I'm not getting anywhere! Surely this is a waste of time.

The first thing to understand is that if something is coming up, it quite simply means that there is more to feel and understand about it. It would not be there otherwise! So no matter how many times you think you have explored something, if it really is there in your experience, there is more to discover.

It is also good to understand that, as we journey with inquiry, deep experiences from childhood really do tend to come up over and over in different ways. Often for decades! But if you are truly open and do not assume that you know what it is about, you will find each time that there is something new to discover in the experience. Being open, friendly, and interested will allow the experience to reveal something new. Perhaps the first time you dealt with that experience, it meant working out something about love. But you might find that the second time it comes up, it is not so much about love but rather a feeling of support. And maybe the third time, it is not about love or support but rather the difficulty in being able to relax and let go.

Many issues and inner experiences tend to come up repeatedly, but if we can be friendly and interested and let ourselves explore them in an open way each time, they will lead us deeper and deeper, often to very unexpected places. Each time will bring a new resolution and might subsequently open the door to a new challenge. The attitude of kind curiosity will serve you over and over.

When I did the exercise, I didn't feel friendly and interested at all. I felt really angry and disappointed. What is the point of that?

What was it that you were disappointed about? If you look into it, you might find that you were disappointed that the friendly interest was not there for you. So whatever reaction you have is telling you something about your relationship to friendly interest. What if you just allow the anger and disappointment and wonder what that is about? "How come I'm so angry and disappointed? What is this place in me that is so upset?" If you stay with it, you might find some hurt underneath it. And if you stay with that, you might recognize some history, perhaps a familiar feeling from your childhood. And when you see this hurt little child, whom nobody cared about or was interested in, you might find you start to feel very sorry for them, like you just want to give them a hug and listen to them. You might find that you naturally begin to feel friendly, caring, and interested in them. Simply allowing each step of the reaction—staying friendly and interested, and continuing to explore it—will eventually lead you right back to the friendly interest itself. I am not saying it will follow this exact path—whatever happens will be very personal and specific to you. But, for sure, staying with the experience will allow it to unfold and take you to the treasure at the center. This is exactly what diamond inquiry can do! We will be learning how to explore in this way throughout this book, and this is only chapter 3—we are just starting out! For now, simply do your best to be as friendly and interested in your reaction as you can—see if something about that seems better than trying to push it away!

FOUR

Steadying Yourself in the Water with Kath Meditation

When you are scuba diving in the sea, strong currents might come along and sweep you away. You need to have the presence of mind to locate where you are and which way is up, and learn not to panic and use up all your air. Similarly, in inquiry, in the inner ocean, you might easily be distracted or swept away by strong feelings, whether pleasant or unpleasant, or by the endless chatter of your mind or the sensations of your experience. So it is important to learn how to maintain a certain focus and presence of mind. You need an anchor in the midst of the flow so you do not get swept away. This means developing your powers of concentration, and that is done using meditation.

Concentration meditation is a bit like training for scuba diving by lowering yourself into the water over a big round rock, and then keeping one hand on the rock and maintaining your position above it. There is not a whole lot that you have to deal with in terms of navigating and looking around. Your job is just to stay above the rock, to practice keeping yourself in one spot and breathing in a relaxed way while you are in the water. Fish might swim by, the waters may be surging or calm—it does not matter. The water conditions do not change your job, which is simply to keep with the rock whatever else happens to be going on.

Sometimes you might drift away from the rock because you were not paying attention to it. Maybe some current carried you off a bit, or you got interested in some sea creature that swam by. As soon as you realize this, you swim back to the rock. You can check out the sea creatures later, when you are actually exploring. But when you are practicing your stability, it is important to practice just that. You will be able to explore more effectively later on if you build your stability now.

Some days the water might be still, and you will effortlessly stay with the rock. Some days the water will be turbulent, and you will continually have to swim back to the rock, unable to stay there for more than a few seconds. Some days the water might be full of fascinating creatures or threats of a shark below. It really does not matter what the water conditions are, and it would obviously be impossible to try to change or control the water conditions. Your job is to practice staying above your rock whatever the circumstances, so that in time you can do it under any circumstances.

Moving to the inner ocean, the focus that you will use—the rock—is the immediate sensation of your lower belly. It is centered on a spot a few inches down from your belly button, and about an inch inside. This spot is recognized as a significant point in many spiritual and martial arts traditions, and goes by many names, including the Hara or Tan Tien. In the Diamond Approach, we call it the *belly center* or the *kath center*.

In the meditation, your job is to attend to the sensations of this part of your body, simply staying in touch with them as continuously as you can.

Your attention may get pulled into something you are thinking about or feeling, or it might be drawn to noises or distractions around you. These are like the currents or fish in the water. If and when you notice that happen, simply bring your attention back to sensing your belly, just like swimming back to the rock.

You are not trying to stop the thoughts, feelings, or other sensations at all. You are not trying to calm the sea or get rid of the fish. You are practicing not letting them take you away from your rock and coming back to it whenever you do get pulled away. You are staying in touch with the sensations of the breath in your belly, whatever else may be going on. It does not matter how many times you have to bring yourself back to sensing your belly in a period of meditation—what matters is that you do so as often as you need to, whenever you become aware that your attention has drifted off to other things.

Sensing your lower belly means just that: you are directly, palpably, in touch with the actual sensations of your lower belly as it expands on your inhale and relaxes on the exhale. It really does not matter *what* you sense there. It could be the sensation of your belt, the warmth of your hand against your belly, or the movement of your belly wall. It could be a cramp, tingling, heat, energy, presence, emptiness, or even nothing at all. It might feel like a volcano, a dark lake, or a mini universe. Whatever you sense is fine. What matters is that you stay sensing it as best as you can.

The meditation has the openness of inquiry. You are not trying to change your inner condition or make anything particular happen. It does not matter what state you are in when you start, nor when you finish. The inner ocean can be doing whatever it likes—there might be fish thrashing around or waves pounding, or it might be totally still and silent. Regardless, you are simply practicing staying focused on the felt sense of your belly with whatever else is happening.

A short period of this meditation—perhaps five minutes—before you inquire will support your inquiry practice. Once a day, a longer period—say, twenty minutes—is optimal, if you can. Occasional practice up to forty minutes every so often is even more beneficial, if and when you can manage it.

EXERCISE: KATH MEDITATION

As part of your preparation for inquiry, take a moment to remember the attitude of friendly interest and then do a short meditation. Set a timer for your chosen period of meditation. Find a comfortable upright sitting position in a chair, or on a stool or meditation cushion if you like. Unlike inquiry, meditation involves a particular posture, although the aims are the same: to allow your body to be awake and alert, without falling asleep or creating unnecessary distraction and discomfort. If you are in a chair, ideally find one where you can have both feet flat on the floor with your knees slightly lower than your hips, supporting you to feel grounded. Feel the contact of your feet on the floor and your butt on the chair. Let your spine be upright and relaxed. Let your chin dip very slightly forward, slightly lengthening the back of your neck. Have your jaw relaxed and your tongue resting on the top palate just behind your top teeth. Let one hand rest in the other, and then rest both of them over your lower belly or in your lap.

Begin to sense the movement of your belly as you breathe. As you get in touch with those sensations, bring your focus particularly to your lower belly. Sit for the practice period, keeping your attention focused on the immediate sensations of your lower belly moving with your breath.

Whenever you realize you have drifted off or got caught up in thoughts or feelings, simply come back to sensing the immediate sensations of the breath in your lower belly, or your kath area itself.

USING A TIMER TO SUPPORT YOUR PRACTICE

If you struggle with concentration, there are ways you can practice building your capacity by using a timer to support you. Many meditation apps will let you set an "interval bell" to ring every so often through your meditation period. Begin setting it for a very short interval, such as one minute. The bell will ring every minute and remind you to come back to sensing your belly. When you find you are easily able to stay in touch with your belly for most of the minute-long intervals, you can lengthen that period by increments of, say, thirty seconds. Meditate at the new interval until you are comfortably able to remain in touch with your belly for that period. Then increase it again. Eventually you may be able to sit for the full twenty minutes with only one interval bell, or even none. Then you can dispense with the external support and continue developing your internal concentration.

Remember that the aim is not to be totally quiet but only to remain in touch with your belly. When you are more practiced at concentration, you might find you can stay in touch with the sensations of your belly in a continuous way even when your mind is chattering away or your feelings are all over the show.

Question and Answer: Kath Meditation

I get distracted by my thoughts in the meditation. What should I do?

As soon as you notice that you are caught up in your thoughts and have forgotten your belly, you just come back to sensing your belly. It really does not matter how many times you have to bring your attention back to sensing your belly during the meditation period. Doing it a hundred times is not a bad meditation. The trick is just to keep practicing doing it as soon as you become aware that you have lost your concentration.

Can I visualize a golden ball in my belly?

Sensing the movement of your breath in your belly doesn't mean thinking about your belly, imagining your belly, or visualizing something in your belly. It means attending to the actual physical sensations. You may also perceive what is in your belly in other ways—for example, seeing something there. That is fine, but it is not the focus, nor is it something you need to do or create.

I have been meditating using guided visualizations. Can I use these before inquiry?

Only certain kinds of meditation directly support diamond inquiry. Meditations, affirmations, visualizations, or guided meditations that actively try to change your state have a different orientation to diamond inquiry and can be less helpful. You are welcome to do them, of course, but they will not replace the value of the kath meditation in developing your stability. You can certainly use diamond inquiry after you have done any kind of meditation, to explore the effects of those meditations, but they are not the best supports for diamond inquiry as such. The kath meditation specifically supports the practice of inquiry in an important way by developing your capacity to remain steady and focused on a felt-sense element of your inner world while being open to anything else going on.

I am in a Diamond Approach group and we are using a different meditation. What should I do?

The meditation practice within an ongoing Diamond Approach group evolves over time, with different styles of meditation depending on what the group is working with. You can use whatever meditation your group is currently working with.

My inner critic gives me a hard time about being poor at meditation. What should I do?

In the period of meditation, you maintain the practice: just keep coming back to sensing your belly, whatever the inner critic is saying. Outside of the meditation, it would be good to inquire into your inner critic, and if you are familiar with the practice of disengaging from the inner critic, you can practice that. You will learn a bit more about the inner critic in chapter 9 of this book, and there are references for exploring it further in the resources section at the end of the book.

All kinds of interesting feelings/sensations/thoughts come up in the meditation, and I want to inquire into them. Can I do that?

The practices of inquiry and meditation are quite distinct. When meditating, practice concentration and keep coming back to the belly; do not actively inquire, no matter how tempting it might seem. You can always take some time after your meditation to inquire into whatever it was that was coming up. There is no need to worry about remembering it after your meditation—if something is important, it will come back at a later time for you to explore, even if you cannot remember it right away.

My experience continues changing and unfolding as I meditate. Should I try to stop that?

There is no need to do anything to your experience during the period of meditation, just like there is no need to try to change the water conditions as you try to stay with the rock. If your experience keeps changing by itself, that is fine. You can let that happen, but do not directly make it the focus of your attention. For example, more experienced practitioners may find some understanding about their experience happening spontaneously while they meditate. This is not the same thing as actively putting your energy into inquiring. Your attention and energy remain simply on attending to your belly. The rest is left to get on with itself however it does. If you find yourself actively engaged with anything happening in your experience, you come back to sensing your belly as soon as you notice that.

FIVE

Entering the Ocean with Sensing, Looking, and Listening

You have done some preparations to go diving, you have dipped your head into the water to take a peek, you have practiced staying steady. And now it is time to get fully into the water.

All introspective or spiritual practices invite you to connect with your inner world, each in its own particular way. The unique power of diamond inquiry comes from combining several fundamental elements. So far, we have started with an attitude of friendly interest and practiced being steadily focused. The next element is to be as in touch with your experience as you can be, live and in the moment. Being in touch means that you are really *in* your experience. You are not lying on the beach looking out at the sea. You are not sitting at home watching a video of someone else diving. You are not swiping through photos of your diving trip from last year. No, you are getting right into the water to explore for yourself.

Getting in touch is the crucial foundation. There is no inquiry without being in touch with the immediacy of your experience. This is so important that it is worth repeating: *there is no*

47

inquiry without being in touch with the immediacy of your experience. You can think about or analyze your experience as much as you like, but if you are not consciously and palpably in touch with what you are exploring, or you do not become more palpably in touch during the course of the exploration, there will be little or no transformation. You will at best add a few more thoughts and ideas to your repertoire. The true power of inquiry to reveal your deeper potentials will remain hidden.

You encounter your experience always in the present moment—the now. You can sense, feel, and know what is happening now because it is here; it is actually happening! It is in your awareness, arising in your consciousness. It is your experience in the moment, in the now. You inquire into your inner world by immersing yourself in the experience of this flowing and changing moment. You explore what is here in your experience so you can begin to develop that diamond-like clarity about what is actually going on.

The easiest way to practice getting in touch is to connect with a part of your experience that is recognizably in the present, and you will use the immediate sensations of your arms, legs, and senses for this. These sensations are actually here, they are really present. Being in touch with the immediate flow of these sensations is immersing yourself in the water of your inner sea. It takes you from floating on the surface to fully submerging.

EXERCISE:
SENSING, LOOKING, AND LISTENING

Begin by remembering the attitude of friendly, curious interest— "Hmm . . . I wonder what I'll find today . . . ?"

Now I am going to walk you through the practice of sensing, looking, and listening. You can do this in several ways. You can read each paragraph and then take some time to do what it says. The resources section at the end of this book contains references to online audio guidance for this type of exercise.

For this first time doing the practice, find a comfortable sitting position, perhaps in a chair with your spine upright but relaxed and your feet on the ground. I suggest you begin with your eyes closed, though they do not have to be.

Start off noticing how you feel now as you start. And take a breath with whatever is here.

Now let your attention go to your right foot and start getting in touch with the immediate sensations of that foot. What do you sense there? Bring this curious, interested, wondering attitude—"What do I sense in my foot?"—and let yourself sense and notice what sensations are there.

Maybe you sense the pressure against the ground, or perhaps your foot touching your shoes or socks. Maybe you can feel the muscles or bones, your toes, the sole or heel of your right foot. Maybe you sense nothing there—that is fine too. If you sense nothing, then just stay with it; keep intending to sense your right foot and feel the absence of sensation. You are just being open and getting as in touch as you can with whatever is there, noticing what you find.

Now let your attention come to your right lower leg—ankle, shin, calf, and knee. You are not thinking about your lower leg or visualizing it but wondering about and tuning in to the living sensations of whatever you find. It can be almost like the very cells of your leg are coming alive and sensing themselves, sensing what is there. Maybe some pain or tension, or a pleasurable sensation. Just be curious, open, and in touch.

Take some time with your right knee and then sense up your right upper leg, slowly moving into your inner thigh, your outer thigh. Gradually move into your right hip. And then sense your butt on the chair. Perhaps you can sense your clothing or the weight of your body sitting through your pelvis on the chair. Maybe heat or tightness. There is absolutely no right or wrong here. Whatever you sense, you are just in touch with that.

Now sense the whole of your right leg from your toes to your right buttock, feeling the sensations of the whole of your leg.

After a moment, let your focus shift to sensing your right fingers. What are those sensitive fingertips with millions of nerve endings touching? Sense your right hand. What temperature is it? Maybe you sense energy. Maybe you can even sense the space around your hands, beyond your hands. Be open to whatever you find. What is there?

Sense your right forearm and elbow. Every time you do this, it might be different. Your experience has literally unlimited possibilities, and that includes your experience of your body.

Sense your right upper arm and shoulder. How is your right shoulder today? Tight and contracted? Broad and relaxed? No need to change anything. Just notice and sense.

Now include the whole of your right arm from fingers to shoulder, and take a moment with that.

Next, we will move down the left side. So let your attention come across from your right shoulder to your left shoulder. It might be quite different from the right, so be open as you get in touch with whatever you sense there.

What is happening as you sense down your left upper arm to your left elbow?

Gradually come down to your left wrist, hand, and fingers.

Maybe it feels like a hand; maybe it does not even feel hand-shaped at all. How do you sense your hand when you are not assuming anything about what it is?

Then sense the whole of your left arm from shoulder to fingers.

And come to your left buttock, your left hip. Notice the breadth, the contact with the chair. Come alive to whatever sensations are happening in this part of your body. Sense down your left upper leg, down your thigh to your left knee. And down your left lower leg, your shin and calf, to your ankle. Then sense the heel and sole of your foot, and your left toes . . . the contact with the ground or your shoes. And then the whole of your left leg from the hip to the toes.

And to round out the sensing part of the exercise, sense both arms and both legs, and open to the sensations of your whole body. You are a bit more in touch with the immediate, tangible, and palpable experience of your body, whatever those sensations might be. Sensing helps orient you to this immediacy, and this immediacy of experience is the ground of inquiry.

How is it for you to connect with your body like this? How does it affect you? Maybe you are feeling calm or anxious or bored or delicious all over—just notice. If you find yourself thinking, "Oh, I know what this is, I've done this before," see if you can notice that idea but not entirely go with that assumption, and be open to the immediacy of what is here now, today.

Sensing orients you inward, and now we are going to start including the environment. As slowly and gently as you need to, let your eyes begin to open. Begin looking, with the same attitude, wondering, "Hmm . . . how is this?" Let the sights come to you. Be open and curious, allowing yourself to be as in touch with your visual perception as you can be. Notice the colors, textures, objects, light, and space around you. You are seeing what is really here, what is really present: the immediate, tangible visual experience in your consciousness of what is around you.

How is your vision? Is it dull and flat or vivid, awake, and three-dimensional? However you find it, remember that friendly attitude, welcoming and noticing whatever you find.

So now you are sensing and looking. Finally, begin to include listening, tuning in to the soundscape around you. Perhaps little background sounds, perhaps louder sounds, perhaps the sounds inside you. Perhaps you can hear the silence under all the sounds. How is it to be really in touch with this, to tune in to the immediacy of the sound? Notice how that affects you and take some time to be listening in this active way.

And now you are sensing, looking, and listening. You are more in touch with the immediacy of what is happening, inside you and around you. This is the practice of being present.

Here are a couple more observations around what you may find. First, notice that the experience is not constant. It is not that you sense your hand and find, "Oh, that's what it is," and then you are done. "That's my hand. Full stop." If you stay attending to your hand, you might feel one part a bit more, and then another. As you stay with it, perhaps you feel more of the temperature, or something else intensifies. So there is a flow. It is just like watching a coral reef under the water, with the fish lazily swimming around; one comes into view, then another, another . . . then perhaps a sudden flurry of activity, then they all disappear . . . Similarly, as you are sensing, looking, and listening, you sense one body part, then perhaps some sounds come into focus, then maybe something more visual, then another part of your felt sensations. Suddenly a feeling of delight bubbles up in your chest. This "now" is a living flow of experience, and you are immersing yourself in that flow.

You might also notice that the more you focus on an element, the more you begin to experience it—that is just how your consciousness works. If you focus on your foot, then bit by bit you begin to sense more of what is happening in your foot, without trying to make anything specific happen. The experience starts magically opening up, revealing more. The longer you spend sensing it and noticing what you sense there, the more you discover!

This flowing, open stream of your consciousness is what you explore in diamond inquiry. Maybe you can begin to glimpse that sensing your arms and legs, looking and listening, is the doorway to much, much more than what you usually think of as simply your arms and legs!

STAYING IN THE WATER

You can meditate on a cushion or do yoga on a mat. Both require specific times, places, and circumstances. But you can sense, look, and listen any time and any place in your life. This is the great gift of this practice. You do not need to be in any specific place or position. Although it is nice to do this slowly with your eyes closed, that is not required. It is a spiritual practice that connects you with your inner world, with your consciousness, and with something broader than your usual habitual thinking or feeling patterns. And you can use it any time or all the time. Sense your arms and legs on the bus or as you drink your coffee or brush your teeth. Sense, look, and listen as you talk with a friend or sit in a meeting or have dinner with your family. Keep immersing yourself in the flow of your felt experience throughout the day. This is an invitation to continual contact with that flow of experience.

Sensing, looking, and listening is a particularly good practice first thing in the morning. Take, say, five to ten minutes to start your day sensing your arms and legs and body, then looking and listening. This will engage your whole body, brain, and nervous system, enlivening your whole psyche and everything in it. It will wake you up to the magic of the inner world. Feel free to use the guidance in this chapter to take you through sensing, looking, and listening until you feel comfortable to do it without.

Sensing, looking, and listening is also a particularly good way to transition out of your meditation. So you could sit doing the kath meditation for a few minutes, and then sense, look, and listen to expand your awareness from the concentration on the belly to include your body and the world around you.

See if you can continue sensing, looking, and listening as you read this book.

In time, you will find that sensing, looking, and listening into the flow of your immediate experience will bring you more fully into your whole life, not just into your arms and legs. The whole inner ocean starts to be available in all of your life. You will be more present in everything. And as you are more in touch with this stream of your experience of your life, you might start to get curious about something or other! So the living flow of experience becomes the material for your inquiry and discovery. Sensing, looking, and listening immerses you in the water of experience and opens up the whole ocean for exploration.

Between now and the next chapter, do the sensing, looking, and listening practice first thing in the morning and then more informally a couple of times throughout the day. Once a day, also take ten minutes after sensing, looking, and listening to continue noticing what is showing up in your inner world: what is on your mind, what you are feeling, what is going on in your sensations. Continue noticing whatever is there.

Question and Answer: Sensing, Looking, and Listening

How do I use sensing, looking, and listening in inquiry?

Throughout your inquiry, you can come back to sensing, looking, and listening, to check in with what is really present here and now, especially if you find you have got a bit caught up in thoughts or feelings and lost touch with your sensations.

I can't feel anything in my arm when I sense it. Am I doing something wrong?

The absence of sensation is itself a sensation. So if you cannot sense anything in some part of your body, nothing is wrong. Simply try sensing the nothingness itself.

When I sense into my body, the sensations distract me from what I want to think about or what I am feeling. Can I skip the sensing, looking, and listening?

Your sensate experience of your body is an integral part of your experience and a crucial source of information for inquiry. It is not really possible to get far with inquiry without including the felt sense of the body. If the practice brings up difficulties, these can be explored further with inquiry. What happens to your feelings or your thoughts when you *also* sense your legs? With practice, in time you may find your way toward expanding your awareness to include your thoughts, feelings, and sensations all at once. These are just different facets of one whole you. All are necessary, so hang in there with the practice!

Is the sensing, looking, and listening practice the same as a body scan?

It has some similarities to the body scan, but sensing, looking, and listening is intended more as an ongoing practice. While you can take some time to deliberately tune in with the formal practice, the intention is to also be sensing your arms and legs, looking, and listening as you go about your daily business in various ways.

Why don't we include the torso in the sensing?

The experience in the center of the body—pelvis, belly, heart, and head—tends to be more intense. As we move from sensing, looking, and listening into inquiry itself, we include these other parts. But in building the basic capacity to be present and in touch with the immediacy of our experience, the arms and legs are what is needed.

CONCLUSION

The three preparatory practices we've covered in part one are all deeply supportive of diamond inquiry. You will notice that they all involve an orientation that does not try to change your inner experience in any way, and they are all entirely agnostic about the content of what you are experiencing. The friendly, interested attitude; the ability to remain concentrated on the sensation of your belly; and sensing, looking, and listening all apply to whatever is going on in your experience. You might be happy or sad, angry or excited, dozy or hungry, clueless or afraid of missing out. You may have a brilliant insight, a deep spiritual realization, or be stuck in the mud of your ego. It really does not matter. You can always be friendly and curious about whatever is arising; you can develop your concentration on your belly in the midst of whatever is happening; and you can be present with your experience sensing your arms and legs, looking, and listening.

And now that you have done all that, you are ready for the main event . . . you are ready to begin exploring!

PART TWO

———

Into the Ocean

SIX

Checking In to Find Where You Are

WAKING UP

Inquiry involves a kind of waking up to where you are internally. Much of the time, most people are only partially aware of what is happening in their inner life, and sometimes even totally unaware. We might go through life only dimly feeling, sensing, or realizing what we are experiencing. Occasionally, when it gets really intense, we might notice it—for example, if we are immensely happy, really angry, deeply peaceful, or strongly opinionated. Otherwise we might only have a vague sense of feeling "kinda good" or "kinda not so great" or "kinda OK," if we notice anything at all. This is like swimming through life with a foggy pair of goggles on. You miss all the beauty and wonder that might be there to experience because you are simply not seeing it.

When you are not awake to it, the inner world runs in the background. You seem to go about living your life oblivious to what is happening inside. You might be running on autopilot, doing what you do through the various routines of your life. Often you are going over the same territory, having the same or similar experiences over and over. It is like you are caught in a current that pushes you back and forth between a few limited spots, or around and around, caught in an eddy and not really going anywhere. Because you are not paying attention and seeing where you are, you cannot really tell what is going on, never mind where you have come from and where you might be going.

Waking up will allow you to start seeing where you are, what is going on, and where you are stuck. Then you can begin to recognize that there is mud in the water or that you are going around in circles, all of which is the first vital step toward more freedom. In order to wake up, you have to stop splashing around on the surface and begin to pay attention to the inner world, to the currents and creatures beneath the external. You have to take some time to look and see where you are and what is going on internally. You need to inquire.

So one of the reasons to wake up is to really experience your life and to live your life fully. You cannot live it fully if you are swimming around with your eyes closed.

TRUTH

You ride out over the water in the little boat and already you're beginning to take things in. The waves are gentle, the sea is a beautiful turquoise, the sun glints off the water. Every now and then you glimpse a flicker of movement in the water below—you're not sure what. The boat slows and stops. Final preparations, and then you pause for a moment, hesitating at the side of the boat. Then you tumble over the side into the inviting water. At first you cannot quite make out what is in the water around you. Then slowly, as the bubbles clear, you begin to take in your surroundings and get your bearings.

Where are you?

When I ask "Where are you?" I do not mean literally—"On the couch, in my living room"—although that might be an aspect of it. I mean, where are you *experientially*? What is going on in your inner world? What is there in your psyche as you begin to check it out? That inner world is alive all the time, even when you are not tuned in to it. Waking up means tuning in and finding out what is here.

You ask yourself, "Where am I? What is up with me? What is going on?" These are all variations on looking around to see where you are in the inner world. You ask this kind of question in an open way. The questions are not like classroom or test questions where you aim to figure out the correct answers. They are not interrogation. They are more open, more like contemplative attitudes or feelings that express friendliness and interest perhaps even without an explicit question: "Hmm . . . let's see . . . where am I? How am I doing? What's going on for me today?" It is just like lowering yourself underwater and looking around in a caring and friendly way to see where you are and what is around.

Then you see what you can say about where you are. You take your time and begin to respond to the interest, perhaps as if you were sitting with the best possible friend. You are simply where you are and take all the time you need to begin to notice and say what is up for you.

The beautiful part in responding to this contemplative attitude or question is that you do not have to make anything up. You do not have to find the right answer. It does not have to be spiritual, special, good, clever, modest, well behaved, appropriate, or any other limitation you might imagine. You can be just where you are and say whatever you can actually say about that.

The friendly interest invites a particular quality that is central to inquiry: it allows you to look for and to recognize and say the truth. You can simply be honest. You are finding out what is true for you—what is true about where you are—and you can do that in the most direct, simple, and immediate way, noticing what you are experiencing. There are many situations where you might be cagier about what is going on for you—and perhaps with good reason! But in the sacred space of inquiry, you have the invitation to just let it all hang out, so to speak, and see and say it how it is. This may or may not be something that feels familiar to you!

So this is not Truth with a capital T. It is not logical truth, philosophical truth, or transcendental eternal truth. This is a very simple, immediate, personal truth or truthfulness of where you are. You are being honest with yourself, and it is what you can recognize as your experience live and in the moment, just because it is quite simply there and real for you. Maybe you are feeling sad about something. You might say that, and you can always check: "Is it true? Am I sad?" Probably you would answer, "Yes, I am!" It is obvious to you because it is obviously true.

So this truth can be anything. Maybe you are thinking about what a great meal you had earlier. Maybe you are sitting there feeling anxious because you do not know how to do this. Maybe you are just feeling very peaceful and nothing much at all is going on. You might be sitting there thinking how stupid this all is. Or you may be feeling yourself as the magnificent vastness of all of reality! Whatever it is, as you check in, you are simply taking time to feel into and recognize whatever is actually true for you.

Your friendly interest invites this simple, honest, and immediate recognition of where you are.

This truthfulness has a particular quality and feeling that you might notice. You can actually tell when something is true for you, right? We sometimes say it has the "ring of truth." You might notice a feeling quality that is warm, reliable, trustworthy, honest. The truth can feel simple and unadorned, straightforward. No bullshit, and no need for it. You are as you are. It rings true and you can feel it. The particular truth of where you are might be painful or pleasurable, but either way there is something about the simple truthfulness of seeing it and allowing it that you can feel, and that feels good.

When you are truthful, you might notice that the waters of the inner ocean take on a particular quality. All of these feelings and effects that I have just described come from this particular quality—the quality of truth itself. This truthfulness is something that our hearts naturally respond to and love; it feels precious and valuable. The inner ocean takes on a warm golden glow that touches your heart. If you follow the feeling of honesty, realness and truthfulness to its source, you might find a particular quality of presence, another jewel of the inner ocean. Warm, real, solid, precious, and reliable; a palpable sense of solid-gold presence, the inner gold of the truth. You will be learning more about how to do this as we go.

Take a moment and try this out for yourself in the moment. See how it is to say a bit about where you are if you could just be honest about it. What is going on for you, right here?

After you have taken a few minutes to do that, notice how it affects you to be honest and truthful in this way. Can you feel the sense of truthfulness? And do not worry if you cannot: you can have it at the back of your mind as something that at some point you might notice explicitly.

CHECK-IN POSSIBILITIES

There are countless ocean situations you might go diving in, from kelp forests to coral reefs, from empty expanses to rocky shores. Similarly, you will come across countless different inner experiences as you check in with where you are. Here are some possibilities for you to be open to.

One Central Experience

Sometimes it is pretty obvious what is up for you: there is one central experience occupying your attention, like a giant ray swimming directly below you as you dip under the water, or a tangle of seaweed that you are trapped in. It might be some particular situation or issue in your life or your inner process that has got your attention clearly front and center. It might be something with your partner or family, something from work, your spiritual practice, the political or environmental situation—it could be any aspect of your immediate living situation. It might be wonderful or it might be difficult. Whatever it is, the point is that there is this one immediate experience that is clearly occupying you in a big way. It is in your world and you know it!

The Past and the Future

Sometimes there is one main experience that is getting your attention but it is something from the past or something about the future. For example, you might still be feeling the residue of an event that happened a couple of days ago, or you might be preoccupied about a conversation you had with your friend earlier. You might even find an event from years ago is in your awareness and having an effect on you now. Sometimes you may find vivid memories or feelings from long ago arising in your inner world now. Or you may find yourself worrying about something that might only happen next year, or at some unknown time in the future.

It is useful to clarify an important misunderstanding about being in the now, and exploring things live. It is true that we always inquire in the present moment and explore our experience live, here and now. Even though there may be events, feelings, or thoughts that concern the past or future, what makes them important and worth exploring now is that they are having a direct and tangible impact on your experience *now*. There is a pull now, a draw, perhaps some emotional feeling or a busyness in your mind, and you are aware of those effects happening right now in the present moment. Being in the now, being present with your experience, does not mean that you should exclude influences or thoughts of the past or the future. It means that you are in touch with and open to *whatever* is present in your experience as you look, which may include influences relating to the past or future appearing for you *now*.

An Inner State

Sometimes you might notice something in your inner world that does not seem to have an immediately clear connection with your outer situation current or past. You might be just feeling contentment or love, or a sadness with no immediately obvious cause.

Multiple Experiences

Sometimes you may find several things floating around rather than only one dominating your awareness. Perhaps a frustration about your work, the peacefulness that came up in your meditation this morning, an ache in your chest, and a concern about your family all show up equally in your experience. So that might be where you are. It is like you are swimming in a busy coral reef with lots of different life-forms around—that just happens to be where you are. You can let yourself notice each of them, give them all space, since they are all here.

Nothing Obvious

I said earlier that it might be really obvious where you are. But, quite frankly, sometimes it is really not so obvious at all! You might have no idea or clear sense of what is going on. You might feel vague or unsure. Maybe the water is not clear—you do not know and cannot feel or sense much. Or there is some unclear sense of something but you cannot yet say what it is. These are all interesting too. If that is where you are, then that is where you are! You can simply be open to and curious about the reality of that experience. What is it like to notice that and hang out with whatever kind of "not much" or vagueness you happen to be experiencing? Remember what happened with sensing your arm or your leg: the more you stay with it and attend to it, the more you begin to notice. It is the same here. So if you start off not in touch with much, or with only a glimmer, then simply stay with that and see what emerges as you do. It can be a relief to say, "Oh, OK, well I just don't know right now. I'm going to hang with that and see what happens." You do not have to make anything up. You can just be with what is real and true in the most immediate sense.

You might notice that just as the preparatory practices are agnostic to the content of your experience—i.e., they are equally valid with any possible experience—this practice also applies to absolutely any kind of content that you might find as you check in. What matters is simply that you are noticing what is up for you, whatever it is, whatever you can tell is going on in your experience and to whatever extent you are able to identify it.

Now that you have some possibilities, check in again. Ask yourself, "What's here?" or "Where am I?" or "What's up with me?" and then take your time and begin to say (or write) what you find. It might take the form of something from the list above or something else altogether.

FOUR ELEMENTS OF EXPERIENCE

As you begin to check in, you will probably find yourself getting in touch with a group of elements that are common to much of our experience. They are often present in deep spiritual experience and also in ordinary day-to-day experience. They are present in experiences of your inner nature, your circumstances, and your history. Your check-in can become more complete if you include each of these different elements.

Your Circumstances

A first element of experience is the life situation or context of your experience—that is, your circumstances. You might compare circumstances to things outside the sea that affect it and stir it up— the weather, the coast, any nearby cities or villages, the seagulls flying above the water, or the volcanos stirring underneath the seabed. Just as all these factors have a direct impact on the sea, different life circumstances bring up feelings and ideas and affect your inner world in various ways. So the particular life circumstances that are affecting you or that come up for you when you are inquiring are relevant, important, and meaningful. Circumstances can refer to any person, people, or situation: your relationships, your family life, your work life, any aspect of your living situation, your hobbies and interests, your financial life, your health, your spiritual practice, or the political situation. Basically your circumstances are aspects of your life or world that you are affected by or connected with in some way.

As you check in, see if some person or situation is "up" for you. You might start with a general awareness of a situation, and you can bring it more to life in your inner world by spending a few minutes talking or writing about the details that feel relevant to you. For example, if it is an interaction with a person, say or write something about the interaction—what happened, what was going on. If it is how you are being affected by something happening in the world, such as a global issue affecting the world or some political events, say something about those events— what is going on and how is it affecting you?

Some people are more naturally focused on the outer circumstances, in which case it might feel very natural to start talking about what is going on. Others are more inwardly focused—for example, being more initially aware of their own feelings. Even so, there might be times when the circumstances are the first thing that comes to mind. And many times the circumstances might not be the first obvious place: you might be more in touch with one of the next few elements, and then you would start there. I'm mentioning these options simply to make space for whatever might happen. There is no need to try to make it go one way or the other, nor any need to make an effort to find some external situation as you begin. As you continue exploring, you will remain open to the possibility that there is some connection with your life and context that you have not yet seen and that might emerge at some point.

The Head Center

The next element you might encounter is your mind, which we call the *head center*. This includes the conventional experience of mind, such as your thoughts, images, ideas, and beliefs. These can appear in many ways. You might have something "on your mind," meaning that your mind is busy thinking about or figuring out what to do or say in some situation. You might be running things over, worrying or analyzing, and trying to understand something in your inner experience or in your life circumstances.

You might notice some idea, belief, or conviction that you have that is being challenged or exposed. This could be some idea about who you are, your life, or life in general: "I thought I was a tough person, but I'm feeling all soft and gentle now"; or "Wow, someone was just really nice to me and that is not what I expected!"

You might find various pictures or images of yourself or of others that appear in your mind, or other kinds of images and imaginations, or memories. These are all aspects of mind.

The head also includes various qualitative experiences of your mind. You might notice that your mind feels bright or sharp, dull or peaceful, agitated or empty. Sometimes you might actually be able to sense these qualities of brightness, or emptiness, particularly if you have done some meditation practice for a while.

We will explore the head center in more depth in chapter 11.

The Heart Center

The third element concerns your feelings, which we often call the *heart center*. Perhaps there is some emotional reaction, such as anger, sadness, hurt, frustration, boredom, irritation, fear, anxiety, and so on. There might be a more positive feeling experience, such as love, joy, satisfaction, fulfillment, kindness, and so on. The feelings that you get in touch with may be obviously connected with someone or some situation, or they may not, or they may not seem so at first.

Sometimes you might find no feeling at all, or some sort of neutral feeling, or a very subtle feeling that is barely a whisper, like the faintest hint of a fragrance in the air. These are all possibilities, and in your check-in you simply want to notice where you are.

We will explore the heart center in chapter 12.

The Belly Center

The last element is what we call the *belly center*, which has to do with sensation or the "felt sense" of your experience. Although we use the term *belly*, the experience could be anywhere in your body. Perhaps butterflies in your tummy or an ache in your head; perhaps lightness in your chest, tingling through your body, or solidity in your core. You might be tensing your shoulders, clenching your fists, or feeling restless in your legs. These are all different kinds of sensations. Some are obviously physical sensations of your body and some are perhaps less so.

Sometimes you might sense some kind of absence of sensation, an emptiness of some kind—perhaps a part of your body that you cannot feel at all. That is an equally valid sensation, so if you come across something like that, notice it and include it. It is just as important as any other possibility.

We will explore the belly center in chapter 13.

Context, belly, heart, and head form a good checklist for checking in to see where you are: "What is going on in my life?

How am I feeling? What is on my mind? What am I sensing?" Finding where you are involves seeing where you are and what is true in all of these elements.

Different people tend to be more tuned in to one element than the others, and it is best to start with what is most immediately there for you, since that is where you are and the truth that will be most available to you. Some people are more emotional and will naturally start with how they are feeling. Some are more about thinking and will start with what is on their mind. Others are more in touch with their sensations. Some people are more immediately focused on their external situations or context, while others are more immediately focused on their internal experience. And it is not always the same—even if you are a head person, one day you might start off totally caught up in some feeling. The point is always to start with the truth of where you are. Your dispositions are also something to be friendly with.

At the same time, it is also important to widen your interest in all of these elements, including any you tend to notice less. They are all part of your experience, and they are not really separate. You cannot get the full picture of what is going on without noticing all of them. If there is a situation happening in your life, you will probably have it on your mind, and you will have feelings about it and related sensations in your body and consciousness. For example, if you have a big day coming up at work, you might have an action plan in your mind, you might feel a little excited and nervous, and you may sense the butterflies in your tummy. If you are in touch with a deep inner peace, then your mind may be quiet, your heart may feel still, your body might be deeply relaxed, and your circumstances may suddenly seem very far away.

For many people, the felt sense tends to be the least available of the four elements, and for inquiry it is particularly important. So whatever your disposition, I encourage you to include your sensations as much as you can.

One last point on pressing pause. When an external situation is "up," some people get very involved in what is happening and in what they want to change about it. Seeing and understanding what you want to change is important as part of your exploration of what is happening. But inquiry is not primarily about problem solving. That is more a surface thing. Inquiry is more usefully about discovering what the situation is bringing up in you or where (in your inner world) you are coming from in meeting this situation. Getting completely caught up in external problem solving is usually a way to avoid experiencing and recognizing how the situation is affecting you. You are to some degree pouring your energy into trying to get rid of some inner experience by managing the external circumstances. Now, it is fine to address the circumstances, but there are treasures to be found by first discovering what the circumstances are activating in you and exploring that.

You can make this explicit when you catch yourself looking too much for solutions by exploring something like: "OK, if that is the situation, suppose I can't do anything about it right in this instant. That is how it is in this moment. What comes up in me? How do I feel about that? How does that affect me?"

And then you can explore the thoughts, feelings, and sensations that are arising as you just land with things as they are, rather than focus purely on what you want to change.

VERBALIZING YOUR EXPERIENCE

Checking in starts with getting in touch with your actual, true experience—becoming aware of it and sensing and feeling it. Then it goes further as you begin to recognize and articulate what is going on in your body, heart, and mind. Many spiritual practices do not explicitly focus on recognition and articulation, and some forms of meditation may even discourage them. But they are absolutely central for diamond inquiry.

Recognition is not exactly mentally figuring it out in a deductive manner, although it uses those capacities. Recognition comes from being directly in touch with the experience. As you palpably touch, feel, and taste your inner experience, so to speak, you will naturally come to see what it is—the experience gradually reveals itself more fully. You might be tempted to start off thinking, "Well, maybe it's this, or maybe it's that," and use logic to identify it based on what you already know or some kind of theory. But inquiry is not about guesswork or speculation. This can be a big relief! You do not have to know anything about your experience other than what you can tell directly from the experience itself! You do not have to fit it into a framework or guess. You can focus simply on what you can really tell immediately from the experience.

For example, as you stay with the experience of feeling happy and keep exploring exactly how it is in the moment—how you feel, how it affects you, how you experience it in your body—at some point it will probably dawn on you what it is about: "Oh, I'm feeling so happy because right now I feel very free," or "This happiness is linked to getting a raise at work and feeling appreciated and seen." And it will be evident to you that that is what the truth is. You will recognize that truth directly from the experience itself. So this kind of immediate honesty and truth is always the focus. Sometimes the best you can say is, "I have no idea why I'm feeling happy right now!"—and that is just the truth of it in the moment. It will be far more helpful, real, and honest to say that, rather than trying to fill it up with theories or ideas about what you might be feeling. And then in the spirit of friendly interest, you do not just get up and walk away: you hang out with it, find out more, and see for yourself. As you do, you allow the word or words that really fit your experience to emerge.

Most importantly, take your time. I remember my own teacher telling me this over and over: "Take your time. Slow down." There is no pressure, nothing that you should or should not find. The more you can simply relax and be open and curious with whatever is there, the better. Take time to get in touch with the experience. Take as much time as you need—and perhaps even a little extra—to recognize and articulate what you are experiencing.

Verbalizing where you are is largely a descriptive affair. It is a bit like taking notes or logging what you encounter in your experience as you go. It is best to be as literal as you can be. You do not need to use elaborate metaphors or try to be poetic or clever in how you articulate your experience, although for some people that comes naturally. You also do not need to use anyone else's framework or words. Feel free to find your own natural voice and your own words for your experience, letting the articulation be the process of you recognizing what you are experiencing as clearly, honestly, directly, and truthfully as possible. You are looking for ways of talking about what is arising that feel natural and true for you and that seem to fit where you actually are.

EXERCISE: CHECKING IN

Begin by remembering your friendly interest. Take a few minutes to sit quietly sensing your belly, and then transition into sensing, looking, and listening.

Then check in. You can check in with your eyes open or

closed, whichever helps you stay most in touch with your inner world. Take ten minutes to look around your inner ocean and explore where you are now. Start with whichever element of your experience comes to your attention first—circumstances, head, heart, belly—and check that out. And then expand your check-in to include all four elements. Check in to see what circumstance or circumstances from your life are up for you in some way. Notice what is on your mind and what the state of your mind is. Feel into how you are feeling emotionally or affectively and what sort of feelings might have been around recently. And check in with your body and the quality of your felt sense. What sensations are drawing you there? You might notice your legs and pelvis, belly, chest and arms, and head.

Take plenty of time to get in touch with the different elements, to recognize where you are, and to find some words that fit and seem true to your experience.

After you have checked in through those various areas, see how you are doing at that point—it is like checking in again, after checking in! The act of checking in might have changed something in you, so you are open to noticing that. How has it affected you to recognize and mention where you are, and to tune in to these various dimensions? How do you feel about it? What do you think about it?

Question and Answer: Checking In

I'm feeling something but I do not know what it is! What do I do?

This happens often, especially when there is something new that you have not verbalized before. Just take your time and hang out with it. Perhaps all you can say at first is, "I do not know what I'm feeling!" Start there! And as you stay with it, give yourself some time and see what else you can say.

What if there are lots of things going on in my experience, not just one thing?

You might very well notice a few things in your awareness: a situation at work, something about one of your relationships, something weird that happened in the meditation, and a curious sensation that you felt in your chest. Begin simply noticing this fact—that there are several things present in your consciousness, just like there might be several types of fish swimming around you in the sea. Then you can let your attention move to what calls it the most.

Does it have to be something happening now? I find myself wondering about something that happened last week or even many years ago.

If when you jump in you find yourself wondering about something that happened in the past, then that curiosity or interest is part of what is present now! Finding what is here now doesn't mean that it literally must be in the room now. It means finding what is present in your consciousness now, which can include things from the past that are drawing you in the present moment.

What if I can't find the right word for what I'm feeling?

This is pretty common, especially if you are experiencing something that is new or that you have not verbalized before. It might take some time to find the word that fits. Feel free to try on different words until you find one that feels closest. Usually when you get it, you will be able to feel it: "Ah yes, that is it!"

Speaking seems to separate me from what I'm feeling. How do I speak and stay in touch with my experience?

For many people, it is not unusual in the beginning to find that when they talk, they seem to lose touch with their experience. It means you are not used to being in touch with what you are sensing, feeling, and thinking, and then verbalizing it at the same time. You will develop this skill with practice—just let yourself go slowly. Experiment with finding a word or two that seems to fit *while* you are staying in touch with your experience. If talking takes you away from your experience, pause, get back in touch, and then try finding a word again while being in touch. With practice you will find your way.

How is articulating different from letting words come in free association?

Articulating your experience is not the same as free associating, or just allowing words to come randomly into your consciousness. Articulating your experience means finding the words that meaningfully express and describe where you are. When you articulate something, it feels real and true; the words seem to fit for you, and they make sense to you. The articulation is very closely tied to the process of recognizing what you are experiencing. You might not know *why* you are experiencing whatever it is that you are experiencing at this point, but your first step is to begin recognizing it for what it is, by finding the words to express or describe it. Some people experience words appearing in their experience, almost as if there is another voice or a source of words that is not exactly them. Then these become something appearing in your mind that you can articulate: "Oh, the words 'come here' just appeared, but I'm not sure what they are about."

INQUIRY AND LIFE

Verbalizing your experience leads to one of the great gifts of inquiry. As you inquire, you are in touch with your experience with presence and awareness, and, at the same time, you are engaging your functional capacities to talk and explore, to write and understand. You are in touch with your inner world as you talk and function normally. For many people who engage in spiritual practice, the depths of the inner world and normal functional capacities can seem to be hopelessly separated. You might be amazed to discover that you can be sitting there, talking or writing in an ordinary way, at exactly the same time as you are describing and experiencing a deep spiritual state, such as a state of no mind or a condition of deep love: "I'm sitting here, and there are no thoughts, just a still, vast silence in my mind that seems to fill the room. Gosh, and as I'm still writing this, even speaking it out loud, the silence is still there. I never thought that was possible!"

When this happens, you can discover that various states of consciousness do not only happen when you are sitting meditating but also while you are doing something rather normal. The very practice of inquiry naturally starts breaking down the barriers between "spiritual states" and "ordinary living." In time, this means that your realizations, your inner discoveries, become far more available to you in a wider range of your life—and far more quickly—than if your only practice was to experience certain states in the simplified conditions of meditation, on your cushion or in a special pose.

Inquiry goes even further to bring spiritual realization into daily life. As you have seen by now, much of what you inquire into arises from the fabric of your ordinary daily life. Your daily life interfaces with the thoughts, feelings, and sensations of your inner experience. Inquiry uncovers, illuminates, and clarifies how every element or difficulty of your life connects with your inner consciousness. Through inquiry, every situation becomes, in time, the doorway to realizing and actualizing some quality or capacity of your inner depths. It might start off looking like you are just exploring some reaction to your partner. But as you inquire, you might begin to become conscious of how the way that you are feeling about them is connected with your whole relationship history, and then with the earliest relating you had with your mother, and then with the deepest inner beloved of your heart, a mysterious hidden depth that calls to you.

These recognitions do not occur by making mental connections or trying to get anywhere but simply by staying with the experience in an interested and curious way and allowing the truth of whatever gets revealed. Most of all, you do not have to take any of what I am saying here on faith. Simply exploring your immediate experience is all that is needed. The rest will happen on its own.

SEVEN

Exploring by Questioning

When you look around the inner ocean to see where you are, chances are good that often you will find a whole lot going on. As you saw in the last chapter, sometimes there is one central experience, like a giant ray underneath you, but often there are a couple of fish over here, an interesting crevice in the rock over there, and maybe a glimpse of an octopus down there, or even a curious glow in the depths farther away. What you see initially as you check in are just the first glimpses of what is in the water today.

If you were swimming and saw a flash of green come up next to you, you would probably not just think, "Oh, look, something over there," and then forget about it. No, you would probably go, "Oh, look! Oh my goodness, what was that!?" You would turn to follow the flash to find out what it is. "Wow, look, it's a sea turtle!" You might then want to follow it, see what it is, what it is doing, and where it goes. You might be captivated for hours trailing this turtle and seeing what it is up to today. And if you explore it with this level of engagement, the turtle might lead you from where it was breaking through the surface down to the secret places it goes.

It is the same with your inner experience. Suppose you feel a sense of something nice. You could just say, "Oh, I'm feeling good," and stop there or keep looking around for something else. But hang on a second . . . what *is* that good feeling? What kind of good are you feeling? "Hmm . . . I don't know . . . It's a kind of . . . feels nice . . . actually hang on . . . it's a feeling of . . . delight!" If you take some time to find out a bit more about it, you can discover more of what it is. It turns out to be a feeling of delight living in your consciousness. As you see that, then you might want to hang out with it and see more about it.

"Hmm . . . what's it like? How does it make me feel?" You could stay with it to find out. At some point you might wonder, "How come it's here? What is delighting me?" Each of these questions is like a contemplating attitude with which you could approach the experience, open to it, feel into it, be curious and wonder about it.

So as you enter your experience and begin to notice what is around, the exploration of the inquiry unfolds through various questions that might arise for you.

Real inquiry has no formula. There is no rule about what questions to ask. Your living curiosity and friendly interest encounter your experience, and the questioning flows from there. It is just like lowering yourself down into the ocean, looking around with curiosity to see what is there, and then finding the direction or the creature, reef, cave, or underwater forest that you want to explore.

Sometimes there are no words. In fact, it often starts in this way. You might simply feel the inquiring attitude toward your experience. You are open, curious, awake, and engaged as you stay with your experience. You look around with this awake interest, and then something catches you and a question begins to form or pops out and your curiosity takes you from there. You may notice one day that this friendly, awake, and curious attitude comes from something even deeper than merely an attitude. There is an open, curious, awake, and engaged *presence*. We will learn more about this in the final chapter.

As you stay with your experience, the wordless wondering can begin to get more pointed as something more particular gets your curiosity. A particular question may gradually start forming or suddenly pop up. You might go from "Hmm . . . what's here?" to "Huh, what's that?!" Here are four initial angles or types of questions that can arise as you hang out with your experience. Each question is like a particular kind of diving maneuver that is needed at that moment. Sometimes you are pulling in for a closer look, sometimes you are sitting back and watching quietly. Sometimes you are kicking furiously to keep up with the creature you are following. As you develop your friendly and curious attitude, you can try out these questions, even if they are not yet coming up spontaneously.

WHERE AM I?

This is the checking-in or locating question we have already looked at. It can take different forms: What is here? What is going on now? How am I feeling now? What is on my mind now? What am I sensing now? What situation is up for me?

All of these questions connect you with where you are now, what is happening in this moment. They begin to pinpoint where in the experiential ocean you are. As you might have seen if you tried checking in after checking in, it is not a one-time question, since where you are is continually moving. At any point during your inquiry, you can always wonder, "OK, so where am I *now?*" Sometimes that is exactly the question that is needed. Again, you take your time and see what is here and true for you now, which might not be what was true for you earlier. Your inner world shifts and changes as you explore, and part of the inquiry is to stay close to this moving and unfolding of your experience.

WHAT AM I CURIOUS ABOUT?

As you begin seeing where you are, the next thing may be to find your focus, to begin zeroing in on what you want to explore. Like the checking-in question, you can feel this in different ways: "What draws me? What don't I know about or understand yet? What catches my interest? What feels important to explore? What is the main thing here?" These questions all allow you to begin finding the direction or focus of your exploration.

You first begin to see where you are, and then you give yourself time to see what interests you, where you want to go. Just like checking in, this is another invitation to find out what is true for you. As you find where you are and notice some initial features of it, what is *your* interest? Where does *your* curiosity pull you? What do you need to discover more about? What feels important to you to look at?

It might feel a little unfamiliar to be guided only by your own interest as you encounter your experience, especially if you are used to having instructions to follow. But it can be very liberating, and, in time, it is the most reliable guide. So I invite you to practice trusting it right from the beginning. You can learn to follow your nose.

There might be times when you do not feel any interest or curiosity at all, and then you might be curious about that: "Huh, how come I'm just not interested in any of what I am experiencing?" When you think about it, that is pretty interesting all in itself. There is something important to explore there.

If you encounter several situations that are "up" in your life, this kind of question might help you find what you most want to explore since you probably cannot explore them all together. You might be drawn to whichever area has the most intensity or charge, or whichever feels most important to you—this is natural and often most useful. And every now and then you might find yourself drawn to explore something that you would not usually look at first—your curiosity might pull you in another direction. The key is to go where you personally feel some draw—whether it is curiosity, interest, or the importance or charge of it. This is just like picking whether to follow the turtle, explore the kelp, or check out that cave down there. And if nothing especially stands out and they all seem equally interesting, then that also tells you something useful. What happens then?

Even if there is just one situation that is up, this kind of question can help you be clearer about what aspect of it you are curious about. The experience might be like a big reef with many different facets and features—sensations, feelings, ideas that you have, and various elements of the situation. You can see where you want to find out more.

At times, the question will not feel needed. The particular experience you want to explore is right there, immediately obvious, and you just dive right in.

When needed, this question helps your inquiry find a direction and focus, which is important. And as you continue your exploration, at various points you might need to come back to this question of "Hmm ... where to now? What am I curious about or what is drawing me about this at this point?" to see where to go from there. There can be many forks on the way as you swim along.

WHAT IS THAT?

Once you have found where you are and what is drawing you, you would swim over toward your focus, for a closer look and feel. You might ask, "Hmm . . . let me see/feel/sense more about that . . . How do I experience that? What is that like? What *is* it?" These are all variations on the same broad type of question.

You have seen that there is a bank of seaweed over there. Now you swim closer to it, hover above it, and begin noticing the shapes, the colors. You see tiny little glass shrimp floating around inside it that you would never have seen before moving in close. And then a fleeting glimpse of a large toothy mouth in the dark crevice on the side. If you stay with it a little longer, you might be able to see some of the distinctive markings on the mouth and realize that there is some kind of eel lurking in there. The longer you stay there and give yourself time to notice what is happening in this little patch, the more you will see. Your inner experience is just like this too, but even more so!

"What is this?" is one of the most useful kinds of questions. You are not assuming that you know everything about your experience—it is certain that you do not! You are moving in closer and inviting the truth of what is there to reveal more. You are giving yourself time to feel, sense, and experience it further, and taking time to verbalize and explore as you go. You are giving the experience time to land, to be there, and allowing yourself to sit with it, and see what gets revealed.

You are interested in what is true, what is there, not in getting a particular outcome. As you explore with this question, you are just seeing what more you can say as you give things some time. There is no need to try to make anything up or come up with a clever answer or draw from anyone else's framework, although frameworks can give you useful pointers to help you recognize what is arising in the experience. But you do not want to try to force the experience into anything. Most of all, you are inviting and trusting what you can tell from the immediacy of the experience itself.

The experience could be a feeling, a thought, a sensation, a situation, or a composite of several of these. Suppose it is a feeling of determination. "Well, what is the experience of determination? How do I experience it? What is it like to feel as determined as I do? Is it a little determination or an immovable mountain of determination? What are the sensations that come with it?" You can hang out with the feeling and explore it in this way.

You can do it with a belief. For example, suppose you recognize that you think people should not act in a certain way. What exactly do you believe about that? What exactly is wrong, and what is wrong about it? You get a little clearer about that belief. Where did you get this belief? How do you know it is true?

These types of questions all help you get clearer on the "what" of the experience.

WHAT'S IT ABOUT?

As you see more of *what* something is, at some point you might start wondering about the why, the meaning: "How come?" You start looking around to see what is making this happen. This kind of question can also appear as: What is making that happen? Why that? Where does it come from? How come that is there? Why is that happening?

Suppose a situation has made you angry. First you might explore *what* anger is, feel the energy and effect of it—that is one aspect of getting to know it. But at some point you also need to know "Well, how come? What exactly is the anger about? What makes me so angry?" And even "Why angry, of all the ways I could react?"

When exploring the meaning of the experience, you are not just looking for a theoretical reason or explanation, although those might come in. Inquiry is not just about analyzing or explaining your experience from the outside in an intellectual way. So saying "I'm angry because of my personality type" or "That's here because my trauma is triggered" or "That's here because of my history with my mother" *might* all be true, but they are all slightly removed from the immediacy of the experience. What really matters is what you can tell from within the experience itself. So you hang out with the anger and you wonder, "Hmm, how come . . .?" And then you begin to see. Maybe in that very moment you find, "Ah, the anger is here because I feel limited. In this moment, right now, I can feel how I am being limited in this situation and that is pissing me off. I *really* don't want to feel limited!" *That* is an understanding arising from the immediacy of your experience. It is not theoretical but directly and experientially true. In the moment that you realize something like that, its truth is quite plainly obvious to you. "Oh, that's what it's about!"

As you stay with the feeling of limitation, you might recognize more: "Oh, this feels just like what my mother used to do! In fact, right now I feel like a teenager, with her telling me I can't do what I want to do! I can almost feel her standing over there!" Then you are seeing the connection with your history not theoretically—"Oh, I think this is because of my mother"—but very immediately and tangibly from within the experience itself. These, rather than merely intellectual explanations, are the kinds of *why* that take your inquiry further.

WHERE, WHAT, AND WHY?

Inquiry is like a dance between these types of questions or contemplating attitudes: "Where am I? What draws me? What *is* it? Why is it here? What is it about?" You can go a long way playing with just these. Remember, I am not trying to give you a magic formula here, but these are like tricks you have up your sleeve, or diving maneuvers that you can use as needed. You can try them out and see what they do, and as you become more skilled in your inquiry, the one you need for the particular exploration will just start coming to hand. The fundamental thing is always your friendly interest in yourself being in contact with the immediacy of your experience.

There are other angles of inquiry that we will touch on in later chapters. But this probably gives you enough to go for a swim—which you might be itching to do!

EXERCISE: SWIMMING AROUND

Begin remembering your friendly interest; and sense, look, and listen. Then check in—with your eyes open or closed—to find where you are, contacting whatever is arising in your immediate experience, seeing whatever is up for you.

After you check in, take a moment to contemplate with interest what is around and then see what draws you in some way.

Then let yourself follow that draw. Move in for a closer look to see more fully what it is, how it feels, and what it is about. Let your interest guide you toward the places that you want or need to explore.

Feel free at any point to stop for a moment and rest. Remember to take your time and not push anything. You can always just check in to where you are at that point and then see where you want to go next. Sometimes there might be a strong momentum pulling you along in the exploration. Sometimes the water might seem a little bare.

Wherever you are, enjoy the ride and the exploration!

Once you are finished, take a final moment to see where you are at the end and how the exploration has affected you—a little check-in to finish off.

Question and Answer: Exploring with Questioning

I'm getting lost with all these questions.

When in doubt, just relax. Take a few breaths, let yourself simply bob in the water for a while without having to do anything, and see what crops up. You don't have to figure it out. After taking some time to breathe, just begin to notice where you are again and then hang out with that and see what happens.

When I check in, there is so much going on that I get overwhelmed and do not know where to start or what to explore. What should I do?

This is a bit like finding yourself in very busy waters with loads of fish swimming around and getting all lost and disoriented. The first thing is to recover your bearings. So one option is to forget everything in the water and simply take some time to get yourself upright again, as it were. You can do this by sensing your arms and legs. Pay attention to the tangible sensations of your hands and feet or arms and legs and don't worry about everything else. This will give you something concrete and tangible to focus on and to ground you. Once you have your bearings again, then you can start exploring and looking around again. Keep sensing your arms and legs. Try looking around a bit, inquire until it seems to be too much, and then simply stop and come back to your arms and legs. If you find yourself getting unmanageably overwhelmed a lot, then it might be good to find some help. (See the resources section at the back of the book for additional support.)

I get stuck a lot and just don't know what to do.
You might get interested in the experience of being stuck. What is happening there? What is making you feel stuck? Sometimes it is because there is something happening in your experience that you are trying to change or get rid of. You might be curious about that. What are you trying to change, and why? What happens if you do not try to get rid of it but instead try to be friendly and interested in it? Also, people often get stuck when there seems to be nothing obviously recognizable around, and they are trying to come up with something. In this case, just let yourself hang out and verbalize the experience of nothing for a while!

You could also get interested in the experience of not knowing what to do. What is it like for you when you do not know what to do? See what that brings up.

I don't seem to have an issue to explore.
Wonderful! Inquiry is most definitely not just about issues, although many people are motivated early on by trying to work

through their issues. Lower yourself into the issue-free waters and explore. What is it like when there is no issue? Does that become an issue for you? Do you feel good? What kind of good? Take your time to see and explore what happens in your inner world when it is not dominated by a problem. This is a very important step, because if you only ever focus on the problems, you will never get to discover anything beyond problems!

EIGHT

Diving Deeper

HOW QUESTIONING TAKES YOU DEEPER

Exploring your experience in the open, interested, and questioning manner we've been discussing naturally takes you from splashing at the surface to diving down into the magical depths. How?

In the ocean of the inner world, the surface is the context: the external circumstances, relationships, and activities of life that are more visible and obvious to us.

When you look a little deeper than the outer circumstances, you come to the thoughts, emotions, and bodily sensations that you have about that situation. These are the contents with which your head, heart, and belly centers are occupied, the conventional experiences that people think of in terms of mind, feelings, and body. This is a next level in, and you have already been noticing it as you check in.

These conventional experiences are influenced by your history through various associations and connections. The way you respond to a particular situation arising now will be based on what the situation evokes in you, and part of what it may evoke are the associations and impressions of similar experiences from the past. Your conditioning and history pervade the inner ocean, shaping the more obvious shallows of your conventional feelings, thoughts, and reactions.

Spiritual experiences and the more profound experiences of life come from even deeper. You could say that these are the very nature of your head, heart, and belly centers. These are the jewels of the inner ocean. You may recognize moments your very depths themselves seem to come forward, when you feel something that touches you all the way through. It might be a deep sense of meaning or fulfillment or connection; a sense of kindness and friendliness or truthfulness and realness that fills your experience; or maybe a sense of power or immense solidity or the feeling of your very aliveness itself. These are some of the qualities of your inner human nature, your consciousness, your beingness, the hidden properties of the very waters of the inner ocean.

We call these qualities of *presence*. They are not ideas or thoughts, not the usual emotional reactions, and not the regular sensations in your physical body. They affect all of those things, and mostly people tend to be aware of those effects at the beginning. But it is possible to go further than these familiar effects—to recognize directly and immediately the presence itself. Presence has an immediate, palpable hereness with all these different qualities. Experientially, it is the very stuff of your consciousness, your human nature in its purity. It is always operating hidden in the depths of the inner ocean. Presence is the hidden treasure that we go diving for.

Inquiry takes you deeper, because all of these levels of experience are not separate, even though you may be unconscious of them at first. They are always meaningfully related and connected. Your outer activities and relationships affect you. You have various related thoughts, feelings, sensations, and urges. As you begin to see what those more inner experiences are and how they are related to your circumstances, in time you might wonder what is making them happen inside you, because it will be obvious that it is not only the outer circumstances. In time, exploring your experience will begin to reveal the deeper layers of your conditioning and your history. Exploring even further will bring you to your inner nature itself, to the recognition of the presence that is always operating at the depths of the experience. So you can take any experience and by staying with it and exploring what it is and what is making it happen, you will begin to follow it from the surface to the deeper, more internal factors, all the way to presence and then back out again. I want to reiterate that describing these layers as being of increasing depth is not meant to imply more or less important, or more or less valuable. They are all important—they are all aspects of what is true in your experience. Our inquiry is simply to see what is really going on and what is true in it.

Here is a very simple example of the different layers. There may be someone in your life whom you love. That is the surface: the life situation, the particular person for whom you feel this love. If you look a little more, you might see you are thinking sweet thoughts, feeling your heart pound a bit when you think about them, or wanting to give them a lovely gift. These are the next level in—the conventional thoughts, feelings, and sensations. You might be a bit worried and tense about whether they love you back, because the last time you felt this way with someone, it ended badly. That would be the influence of your conditioning and your past, shaping how you experience now. And if you were to explore and follow what is making all of those different urges, feelings, and thoughts happen, both the pleasant and unpleasant, what links and underlines the conditioning, the thoughts, feelings, and sensations, you will see they are happening because of *love*. If there was not something in you that could love like this, none of this would be happening! They are occurring because when you think of this person, you begin to feel this palpable, sweet, exquisite, appreciative love that feels like pure "liking"— you like this person so much your heart feels it will burst! The more you explore this experience, the more you will discern that it is a tangible, conscious beingness—a palpable presence—that you can sense, that is pure sweet, appreciative generosity. Your heart in the middle of your chest feels experientially as if it is literally made out of this presence. If you continue exploring it, at some point you might recognize that it is just what you are; it is the nature of your heart! And then you would understand the true source of all the rest of the details of your experience, expressing itself in the relationship in your life. You might see how your conditioning and past experiences have affected the expression of that sweet loving nature in some way. You might see that your loving heart is still there, despite the past, and can survive the losses and heartbreaks of the past. And this recognition will free your loving nature from the shackles of the past.

It is relatively easy to make an intellectual connection that, "Perhaps I feel these urges because I must be loving." That can be an exercise in logic, and it is helpful to open you to possibilities that you might not have considered. It is like thinking that the dolphins eat food at the bottom of the bay, because what else would they be diving for. Maybe it is true; maybe it isn't. It sounds reasonable, but you do not know with certainty without seeing for yourself. With inquiry, you need to follow the dolphin down until it leads you to exactly where it goes—then you really know because you have seen it clearly yourself. So, you land in with your experience as you are having it and then let your curious exploration and questioning explore it. Gradually the experience reveals what is there and what is making it all happen, as you are in it, following it live. In time it will lead you all the way to the truth of presence.

It turns out that you can explore any situation or experience in your inner world, and by diving from the surface to the depths, you can discover some quality of your nature, of presence; a jewel of the inner ocean that is at play. This is a possibility to be open to, which you might not have considered. Using the same kind of logic I just mentioned, you might reason that you are able to be strong in certain situations in your life because somewhere within you there is strength as your very nature. You are able to be intelligent in your life because there is the presence of intelligence. You are able to be playful in your life because an aspect of your nature is the essence of joyfulness. And when you feel the absence of any of these qualities, you miss them because somewhere you know they should be there, and even that is pointing you to their ultimate presence. With inquiry, it is possible to know the truth of your nature not as an idea or logical deduction, but as lived experience. This is not the usual lived experience of most people! Most people do not experience themselves as the pure presence of brilliance and intelligence, or as pure fiery, expansive strength. But you can know your nature in this way.

To discover these hidden treasures, you need to not take things at face value, not stop at the surface or even at the next level in. You check in, you start wherever you are, with what is true for you. You let that truth be your guide and then you explore to see what else you can see. Rather than taking your experience at face value, at the surface level, you question it to find out more and dive deeper and deeper. You need to be getting more and more in touch with your experience and sensing it in a deeper way than simply being aware of your thoughts or your circumstances.

DEEP DIVING TO PRESENCE

It still might not be apparent to you how the exploration might take you in practice all the way to the treasures of the inner world. So here is a fuller example to illustrate the process of taking your experience seriously and then exploring it beyond face value, all the way to the trenches and through.

Suppose you feel an urge to get an ice cream. You could take it at face value and just go and do it. Or you could not take it seriously at all and ignore it. These are the most surface responses. But once you know there might be more to it, you sense, look, and listen, and you wonder, "Hmm, what's going on here?" Now, some days you may find that it was just what it seems! Sometimes an ice cream is just a yummy ice cream and you want one!

But let us suppose that this day, as you check in with your feelings, you realize that actually you are feeling a bit meh. Not great. So now you have seen something more and begun to notice a feeling that was not apparent at first. You get curious about that feeling: "Hmm, what is this?" You pull in a little closer and stay with it, taking your time to feel and allow it. You begin to realize that you feel kind of sad. More is being revealed! You stay with it, wanting to see more of what it is. You notice and feel the exquisite softness, delicacy, and ache of the sadness in your chest. And then you wonder, "Hmm, what am I sad about? Where does it come from?" As you contemplate your sadness with this question, you realize it started earlier in the day during a conversation with your friend, when he said he was going to be busy this weekend, so you would not see him. And you were disappointed. Then you realize that actually you are feeling lonely. Staying with the experience beyond the first glance has slowly revealed more about the what and the why.

Now, you could take the loneliness at face value and just go with that. You could find another friend to visit and maybe even have an ice cream with them! This will be more helpful than just getting an ice cream because it is based on a more accurate recognition of what is going on inside you. So the inquiry has already helped you. Or you could keep diving . . .

Now you sense and feel into the loneliness: "Hmm, what is *this* . . .?" You start to recognize a distinct feeling of something missing, an absence—the lack of company or companionship, the lack of feeling at ease and relaxed and cozy. Now you are going even deeper. You continue, curious and interested even though it is rather uncomfortable: "What is this sense of lack?" You feel lonely and wanting for company, and then comes a clear impression of being young and alone and wanting someone to give you a hug: a piece of your history has appeared. You stay with this experience, inviting it to reveal more of what it is and where it came from, feeling the difficult feelings of the young child you were.

You sense your body deeply, and there is a tangible sense of emptiness in your chest, like a hollow, empty crater. Now you are diving right down into the trenches. It brings wanting, longing, and reaching for someone. As you let all this happen, you realize how you usually use company to fill this emptiness, to take it away so you do not have to feel like a helpless child left alone.

You see the connection between this deeper difficult place from your history and some of what you do now in your outer life. But this time you recognize you are not a child now, and you can allow the deep, dark emptiness. You sense into it, allowing the tears that it brings. You recognize that you feel totally alone, and you let yourself go all the way inside that alone emptiness. As you see this child and feel the feelings, you start to feel something warm and gentle inside you. Seeing your loneliness as a child and feeling this lack, you totally and spontaneously feel an urge to give the child a hug, like you want to wrap your arms around the little child that you were. As you allow the impulse, a gentle warm sensation starts flowing from the depths of the emptiness in your chest like warm, melting honey spreading from your heart through your body. It feels as if the very waters of the inner ocean, of your consciousness, are embracing and hugging you. Your consciousness feels like the very essence of a warm, embracing hug, with an intimate feeling of togetherness and sweetness even though nobody else is around. It strikes you very clearly that *this* is exactly what you have been needing, though it is appearing in a way that you could never have imagined. The tension completely relaxes all through your body.

After some time you realize you do not feel lonely anymore. This sweet, melting, warm golden presence from your very nature itself has responded to your need, taking you through the trenches. You look back at your situation with your friend and you realize that now you *could* see a friend, maybe even for an ice cream, and that would be lovely. But you could just as well be on your own today. It does not seem like a big deal. Both would feel intimate, cozy, and relaxed without a sense of anything missing. You simply do not feel lonely in the same way, and the emptiness in your heart has transformed into a spacious openness, filled with a sense of sweet, warm melting—the very essence of a hug. Usually we associate this feeling with the presence of another, but it turns out it is possible to discover it simply in your presence itself.

This is the dance between finding where you are, following your interest, and exploring the what and why of it more deeply than you might have done before. You get in touch with the sensations, feelings, thoughts, and context, however they are showing up, and then continue to contemplate them, being willing to see more, to go deeper. Each step reveals itself simply as what is true in that moment and with time and curiosity naturally opens and leads you to the next. This takes you from the surface step by step, realization by realization, to the very depths and then back again with a new treasure. It happens not by trying to get anywhere, not by trying to change or fix the problem, but simply by being interested in and exploring what is actually going on as it is happening and by being as in touch with it and sensing it as best you can. In each moment you are simply with what is true in that moment, remaining interested and open with what you can actually say about it and what more there is to see.

You could skip or abort the adventure in so many ways. You could just have gotten the ice cream and not looked deeper. You could have distracted yourself from any of the difficult feelings along the way. You might have told yourself to grow up and not be sad, or that it should not matter if your friend is not around for you. By not allowing each moment its own truth, you would not have found your way all the way to the depths with this sweet, melting presence!

Needless to say, it may take longer—sometimes a great deal longer—than a few minutes to penetrate the experience and understand and open it up all the way to the depths. But this is precisely what inquiry can do with time and practice.

This applies to every possible experience. You can start anywhere and follow it and explore it to the depths, and it will lead you down the trenches to the hidden treasure. You learn to take your experience seriously. Whatever is happening is important and valuable, and also a step and an entry. You give it time, and you feel and sense it as much as you can. You do not have to dismiss, change, or fix anything. *And* . . . you do not take it just at face value. When you inquire, you are willing to keep looking deeper, to keep seeing more about what it is and what is making it happen.

EXERCISE: OPEN INQUIRY

Now you can go out to explore for yourself. Begin by seeing if you can find that friendly attitude toward yourself and your experience. Take a moment to sense, look, and listen. And then once again start checking in with yourself in a relaxed and easy way. Where are you? What is here in your inner experience?

Then see what draws you, where you want to focus. Explore that, being open and curious about whatever comes up. Take your time to feel and sense into the experience and to wonder what it is and what it is about. See what you can tell from the immediacy of the experience. Do not worry if you feel like you do not know what you are doing; just see if you can explore whatever is arising in your experience. You cannot get it wrong!

Explore for fifteen minutes either in writing or by speaking out loud in a monologue.

Do not be surprised if you do not immediately go plunging down into the treasures! You would not expect that of yourself the first time you go diving in the sea, so have the same friendly patience with yourself in the inner world. You might need to paddle around and feel a bit awkward and odd as you learn how to navigate in the inner world. You might get stuck and not know what to do. You will probably kick a bit hard and bump into whatever you are exploring, or go sailing right past it so it disappears from view! It is all to be expected and all an opportunity to learn and practice. Hang in there. Simply explore whatever it is that comes, to see what is true for you at each step.

Question and Answer: Diving Deeper

When I'm inquiring, I notice I start feeling like a child again, stuck in some issue with my mother. I can't believe I'm not over this yet! What should I do?

This is one of the things you will find at some point—it is not a problem and not a mistake. Remember, we are always interested in what is true. So, if it is actually true that you begin to feel something like a child, then that is where the inquiry is taking you. Simply be interested and curious in that child. How does the child feel? What is it like to be with the child? What is going on with them? You can simply be interested in everything about the young parts of your psyche that you might encounter. These parts lie in the deeper reaches of the inner ocean, and inquiry will naturally bring them to light for exploration.

I was doing fine; there was lots coming up. And then it all went quiet. Now I can't find anything. There's nothing going on no matter how hard I try.

This is also definitely something that happens. See if you can be interested in the nothing. What happens if you just hang out with nothing happening for a while and see what you can say about that? It is often the case that after we explore into something that has a lot of emotional charge, the emotions might settle down, and it might feel empty. This emptiness is a very important doorway, so stay with it and see where it takes you.

Can I focus on my childhood?

History is generally not something that you have to go looking for. It will show up as it is relevant, as in the example earlier. Some days, when you check in, you might actually have a particular event or something from your history on your mind or pulling your attention. In that case, for sure you can follow that. What is it? What about it is drawing you? What happened there? As you hold it in these curious ways, see what comes to life in your experience and continue exploring that. You might find you are focusing a lot on the details of what happened. And then remember to check in—to see where you are and what is happening in this moment—as you do so. What are the thoughts, feelings, and sensations that are coming up in relation to this history? That way you keep your inquiry grounded in the immediate experience, which is vital. Just talking about your history is not inquiry. Feeling and exploring directly how your history is shaping your inner ocean right now—that is inquiry.

Are there any traps I should look out for?

There are several things that you might find yourself doing that *can* be part of the inquiry process but that can also be traps if they get out of balance. There are no real rules here, and all of these elements might be appropriate at any given time. But if you find yourself stuck with one of them on repeat, then it may be time to get curious about that and perhaps broaden your inquiry.

- Theorizing about, explaining, or interpreting your experience: It is sometimes useful to try different theoretical explanations for what is happening, if you have a framework that you like or find useful. But hold it lightly. See if you can be most led by what you can directly tell from the experience itself, and trust that over possible explanations that you cannot seem to directly validate from the experience. Just like diving in the ocean, the focus in inquiry is on the live exploration. You can read up on the theory when you are back on the beach, and no doubt it is useful to have some theoretical knowledge to guide your exploration. But the emphasis is on the immediate tangible exploration of what is true in your experience.

- Judging or evaluating your experience: Criticizing or viewing your experience as bad or inappropriate definitely hinders inquiry. We will be exploring more about this in the next chapter.

- Unconsciously acting out your experience: Simply taking your experience at face value and running with it is not really inquiry. This is particularly true with strong emotions that feel very compulsive. We will learn more about these in chapter 9, but it is important to remember that with inquiry, you are building the capacity to be with your experience and explore it, rather than simply charging off with it.

- Trying to change or fix your experience: One of the biggest motivators for inquiry for many people at the beginning is to try to fix something, to change themselves or to make themselves feel better. This is very understandable as we have seen, but in time you will see that the most powerful thing you can do is be interested in what is true and what is going on, rather than trying to get rid of it or fix it.

- Trying to get to a particular state or end point rather than simply getting clear about your experience and understanding it: Having an end goal in mind is a variation on fixing things: "I'm going to inquire to feel love" or "I'm going to inquire to get rid of my ego" or "I'm going to inquire to make peace with this situation." These agendas will block your inquiry. The best thing you can do is simply explore what is going on, what it is, and what it is about. The rest will take care of itself, usually in ways that you could never even imagine. As usual, the way to deal with an agenda is not to try to get rid of it but simply to be curious about it: "Oh, look, I have this agenda! How is that affecting me? What is that about?" It is simply another creature in the ocean. Sometimes just noticing it is enough to unhook it.

- Just sitting silently for an extended time in meditation without active exploration: It might be tempting sometimes to just sink into the silence, and it is certainly fine to do that, if that is what is coming up. But you can take your time and allow that, *and* still continue the inquiry. How is it to sink into the silence? Every now and again, say a few words about how it is to be like that. You will find from one minute to the next there might be subtle changes arising that you can notice and articulate, and you might get curious about them. Or what if you get a little curious: "What *is* this silence anyway?" You might feel your mind is quiet, your feelings are quiet, but where is that coming from? Those are the effects . . . what is making that happen? And see what you can discover about it, without taking yourself out of it. You might wonder, "What is the texture of the silence?" How do you experience it in your body or around or beyond your body? What happens when you feel into that very texture itself?

- Continually jumping from one thing to the next also limits inquiry: We can get stuck in following one fish a bit, and then another, and then another, and then another, and none of it seems to really go anywhere. Now, there is no rule here. Sometimes it *is* relevant to include another fish. So you need to see if it is connected with what you were already exploring, or if some element of the combined experience is important. But if you find you just go from one to the next, and there is no deepening or expansion but just going around in circles, then at some point you know it is time to stop splashing around on the various parts of the surface and start diving more deeply into one experience.

- Telling a familiar story that you already know, in a disconnected way from the immediacy of your experience: After you have been inquiring for a while, you may notice some aspects of your inner world coming up repeatedly. The trick is to remain fresh with it. Try not to just trot out the same old story again. And try not to assume that it is the same thing as before. Approach it fresh and see what is coming out now. It might look the same at first glance, but the more you explore how it is showing up right here, right now, you might discover that there is a new angle in it that you had not noticed before, which may be the magical key to the next treasure. So, as ever, stay close to what is actually happening and trust what seems true as you explore it live.

NINE

The Freedom of Inquiry

THE OPENNESS OF INQUIRY

Diamond inquiry is a practice of profound freedom. When you inquire, you are open to anything that shows up. Your inquiry can become so free that you want to explore the entire ocean of your inner world, from the shore to the deepest trenches, from the giant whales to the tiny plankton. The attitude of inquiry always brings the same curious, open interest to whatever shows up. This openness is expressed in the most basic instructions to get in touch as deeply as possible with whatever is going on and to get as clear as you can about it, to explore and understand your experience as fully as you can. You are open to whatever is there, to feel it, to be with it, to explore it; and you are open to whatever truth emerges.

With inquiry, you enter anything that comes up in your inner world. You cannot get it wrong because wherever you find yourself, whatever is going on, is precisely what you explore. As the old spiritual truism goes, if it is *in* the way, it *is* the way!

THE INNER CRITIC AS A BARRIER TO OPENNESS

Now, that all sounds good in theory. You might think, "The freedom of the whole ocean . . . can't get it wrong . . . just explore . . . who wouldn't want that?"

But after you have been practicing for a while, and maybe even right from the start, you may have some moments where you think it is all going horribly wrong. You might start noticing experiences in your inner world that you think should not be there, that you feel bad about. Your friendly interest may seem to desert you! You might be giving yourself a hard time about what you are finding. It might be something familiar showing up again: "Oh my goodness, not this again! How can I still be dealing with that issue? I thought I had sorted that out years ago!" Or you might find a new feeling that you have not noticed before, that you feel should not be there, such as resentment or desire—heaven forbid! Or you might find that you are getting more sensitive about certain situations; you feel affected by things that never seemed to bother you before. You might also start recognizing things about your circumstances or situation that are not comfortable to see—for example, you might feel bad admitting that, actually, your friend was not being such a good friend the other day, as much as you want to say that they were; or that your job is boring you.

You may also find yourself giving yourself a hard time about how you are doing with the inquiry practice; or the sensing, looking, and listening; or meditation. There might be a voice in your head saying things like, "You're useless! You're never going to get this right! Everyone else is doing this better than you. You haven't a clue! You can't even sense your leg! You just get stuck again. Your mind never stops talking. And look, now there's nothing going on *at all* in your experience. What the hell is wrong with you?!"

You might ask yourself, "Am I OK with this experience that I'm getting in touch with here?" or "Am I open to this experience?" Sometimes the answer is, "Definitely not!"

All these experiences I have just described are uncomfortable. Your openness to your experience and your freedom to explore get limited because you feel bad about what is there. So . . . if you do not get hung up on the undeniable discomfort, you might get interested to explore this phenomenon to see what is going on. This is, after all, a part of what will be true in your inner world sometimes. Perhaps, surprisingly, there is something fascinating to discover even here.

If you look closely at the experience of feeling bad about your experience, you might see that there are two things going on in your consciousness. On the one side, there is the experience that you are having: a thought, a perception, a feeling, a sensation— whatever it might be. And on the other side, there is some kind of judgment or criticism of this experience. There is another part of your consciousness that thinks the first experience is not OK, and it is berating or criticizing you for having this experience! So one part of your consciousness is attacking, criticizing, or judging another part. It is a two-sided conversation, and both sides are within your inner ocean! Pretty much everyone finds this phenomenon at some point when they start looking inside. As you begin waking up and articulating your experience, chances are good that you will notice and feel it more and more.

We call this phenomenon the *inner critic*, the *judge*, or the *superego*. Like anything else in the inner world, it is something to dive into, to explore, and to understand the truth about! It is good to appreciate from the outset that the inner critic can often be an unwelcome companion on the inner journey, from the beginning or sometime thereafter, and on and off for many, many years.

THE ORIGIN OF THE INNER CRITIC

Let us step back for a moment and understand something about the origin of the inner critic. Here is a bit of theoretical understanding that will help you orient and explore it more fully when you are in the encounter.

A real ocean is both an exciting and a dangerous place for a child. Children need protection, perhaps a demarcated area that is safe for them to play in, rules about where they can and cannot go, an eye on them to make sure they do not slip on the rocks or get stung by jellyfish, and a lifeguard to pluck them out the water if they get into difficulty.

The same is true of the inner ocean. Children learn from their parents what parts of the inner ocean are OK and what parts are not. They need the protection of parents and caretakers to keep them from too much frustration or fear; to keep them safe and make them feel warm, loved, and secure. They learn where they can go and where they should not go. They learn what they can let in and what they should not let in.

They take in these rules as best they can, absorbing them from what their parents say and, more importantly, from what their parents do, and what they *allow*. Children learn what they can be open to. Children will often take in limitations that might be realistic and helpful in some situations and, without thinking or realizing it, apply them in much broader ways. For example, children learn not to push other children into the water, which is helpful. But if they are excessively reprimanded for pushing them, then they might pick up not only that pushing children into the water isn't good, but that any energy and boisterousness is bad and should not be allowed in a more general way. Or they might pick up that they shouldn't interact with other children or other people at all to avoid being scolded. They do not have the experience and understanding to be able to pick up the nuances of what is meant. This leads to broad and sweeping prohibitions that can continue to affect and limit us our whole lives, even though we are no longer little children depending on our parents' instruction and goodwill.

Maybe you were encouraged to be good and sweet if you were a girl, or brave and strong if you were a boy. Maybe you took in that it is not OK to be the other way around. Maybe it is good to be smart, but not good to be too clever, too much, or "too big for your boots." Maybe you got a message that it is fine to be loving, but not fine to be lusty and juicy. Maybe you were taught to always be grateful. That sounds nice, but then what to do if something that you were given does *not* feel good for you? You might be stuck feeling bad if you are not grateful! Hatred is generally not at the top of anyone's list of acceptable feelings and yet hatred, too, is something that can sometimes arise in our inner world as children, and now as adults.

So everyone takes in all of these messages about how we should be and what we should do, and how we should *not* be and what we should *not* do. The specifics are very particular and personal to you and your history. These shoulds and shouldn'ts form the nets, walls, and barriers of a little paddling pond or safe zone in the inner ocean. They keep you away from the parts that seemed unsafe when you were a child. They also keep out some of the creatures that might otherwise come swimming in. Whenever you approach the edge of this safe zone, or whenever something forbidden or even simply unknown starts getting closer, the inner critic is like the lifeguard who starts blowing a whistle and yelling. It got the instructions from your parents and now it is going to make sure that you stick to them. If necessary, it will jump into the water after you to drag you out and then yell at you to make sure you never do it again.

This is an amazing mechanism of the human psyche through which you learned how to stay safe within *your* family and childhood environment, and how to keep the love and care that you needed. Your very survival depended on it as you grew up. It kept you in the shallows and away from the rocks, so you did not get hurt, eaten, swept away, or lost. It kept the nasty monsters out. It is a tremendous adaptive capacity that was essential to grow up.

THE EFFECT OF THE INNER CRITIC

But now you are a grown-up. If you want the freedom to swim your whole ocean and discover its treasures, this lifeguard can be a real barrier, and it is something you have to deal with. As long as it keeps you bound by the rules of your childhood, it is a complete constraint to your freedom. It does not let you grow up. The inner critic is only open to what it thinks should be there, to what your conditioning taught you is allowed in the pond. No sharks, no dolphins. It probably cannot even tell them apart anyway. No adventuring in caves or skinny-dipping at night.

The inner critic has a whole bag of tricks to keep you in the little pond. It makes you feel bad or guilty or ashamed for experiencing anything it thinks you should not. Guilt and shame to make you feel devalued and shrunk down are some of its favorite tools. You might find yourself in an endless dialogue in your mind trying to explain or justify yourself, in a way that somehow never quite does the trick. The inner critic takes away your energy, your zest for life. It traps your open, inquiring spirit and you end up feeling lifeless, depressed, heavy, and dull. If you notice any of this happening at any point in your practice or in your life, you might start to wonder if your inner critic is at play.

One important distinction that the inner critic does not know about is the difference between experiencing something and acting on it. Remember that with inquiry, you are pausing the action so that you can look into what is arising within you, in order to go deeper. For example, the inner critic might want to keep you away from feeling and knowing your heart's wishes, because it thinks if you allow your heart's wishes, you will do something stupid or not be able to follow them anyway, so what's the point! But we are not talking about acting on all your wishes here but rather allowing the wish so that you can explore it to discover what it is about, what is making it happen, and what is true there. You do this so that you can continue deeper toward the hidden treasures of the inner ocean.

As you've learned, every experience is a doorway to some truth and some treasure. But if you cannot allow the experience, or you feel very bad when you do, then it will be hard to explore it. Think back to the example in chapter 8: at each step you could imagine a judgment that might stop someone from going further. You shouldn't think about ice cream, it's not on your diet! You should not feel miserable—you should just think happy thoughts! You should not be so sensitive about your friend! You should not need your friend to be OK! You should not feel empty and sad! You should not cry! You should not feel young like a child! You should not feel nothingness in your chest! You should not feel melting and soft—pull yourself together! You should not feel totally content to be on your own—you need other people! Just notice for a moment how it affects you to read through that list of prohibitions! Every step could be sabotaged by some kind of judgment that pulls you out of the water and shuts the exploration down, and yet exploring the truth of each step is what allows the next step to be discovered.

How do you spot the inner critic? Look out for the kinds of feelings, thoughts, and sensations described above—that is a good start. It will probably not be exactly like that for you; your inner critic will have its own flavor and forms. But hopefully you get the general gist of it.

Another useful way to identify the inner critic is to ask yourself, "Am I OK with this?" with whatever you happen to be experiencing, or "Is it OK for this experience to be here?" If the inner critic is engaged, then you will feel that somehow you are bad or wrong for having this experience. It will feel like it should not be there, and you are not really open to it because it should not be there. There is a sense of some judgment or criticism that makes it hard to be with the experience, and it pushes you away from it. The experience itself might be positive or negative, but if you are able to be with it, and it feels OK for it to be there, as if there is nothing trying to take you away from it, then your inner critic probably has not "got you."

The openness and freedom of inquiry are guaranteed to activate the inner critic. Sooner or later, your exploration will take you to the edge of the pond or beyond, or start opening up the walls to let some interesting and wilder creatures come swimming into your psyche. It just will. It is good to be prepared for this, so you do not get caught by surprise. When you come to the edge, your inner critic will probably go bananas, blowing the whistle, sounding the alarm, and making you feel terrible about what is happening. So it is essential to learn how to deal effectively with it. Some people get stuck for years not really moving in their process, because they are being made to feel so bad about whatever is appearing that they cannot land there and let it open up.

The good news is that it is possible to work with it! Disengaging from the inner critic is a whole skill in its own right. When you start experiencing it as a real barrier, there are courses and resources (see the resources section for some ideas) that can support you in wising up and practicing.

The first thing is to wake up to the possibility of the inner critic, to recognize when it is limiting the freedom of your inner world. If you do not recognize it when it is active, it will simply stop your journey in its tracks. You will not be able to get in touch with or continue exploring whatever is showing up because you will feel too bad about it. You will keep getting dragged back to the pond or onto the beach.

EXERCISE: SPOTTING THE INNER CRITIC

Here are some exercises to look into the freedom of inquiry and what limits it. This is a particular type of inquiry that is useful for exploring new territory. It is a bit like shining a flashlight into the unknown waters at the edge of your familiar territory to get a sense of what might come bubbling up from beyond. We call it a *repeating question*. This exercise includes three questions or prompts that you will go through one by one.

You will contemplate a question and just let an answer come to mind. Just reply spontaneously with whatever pops up—a sentence or two or three at most, not more. When you have done that, take a second or two to give yourself a little space and then ask yourself the question again. See what pops up then, again in a spontaneous manner. Keep doing this, repeatedly asking and answering the first question spontaneously for about ten minutes, then move on to the second question, asking and answering that one for ten minutes. After that, move on to the third question.

If you are doing this with someone else, you could ask them the first question for ten minutes, and they could ask you the same first question for ten minutes. Then you could ask them the second question for ten minutes and then they ask you the second question for ten minutes. And so on.

1: "Tell me something you shouldn't experience."

You might say, "I shouldn't be too full of myself" or "I shouldn't be needy" or "I shouldn't make mistakes" or "I shouldn't be attracted to that person." You are inviting yourself to see things that your inner critic will push you away from, which might limit the freedom of your inquiry. You could also take some time to look at things that you *should* experience, basically the inverse of the question, to which you might answer, "I should be kind" or "I should be on top of things."

After contemplating and repeatedly responding to that first question for some time, take a breath, sense your arms and legs, and notice how you're doing. And then move on to the second one.

2: What is right about limiting the freedom of your experience with shoulds?

Obviously some part of you thinks this is a good idea, or you would not be doing it! Again, just answer spontaneously: "Well, if I wasn't limited by these shoulds, I wouldn't know what to do or how to behave." "I need these shoulds to keep away those horrible feelings." "Damn right I shouldn't be doing that! People would just run around like animals if they didn't have these rules!" Just keep exploring the reasons that you think the shoulds are necessary. You might get to a point that you think, "There's nothing right about limiting myself with these shoulds!" and if that comes up as your answer, then say that, just like any other response. So you can always answer spontaneously with whatever comes, even if it is something you have said before and it arises again.

And now a final question.

3: Tell me something you are open to experiencing now.

Once again, just allow whatever comes up, including your lack of openness! It is probably true that your inner critic doesn't completely constrain your inner world—there are many things you are open to experiencing. Having recognized some of the things that have been off-limits, you might be surprised to discover what you are now open to experiencing.

And at the end of the exercise, take a breath and a moment to check in. Notice where you are now, how you are feeling, and how the exercise has affected you.

Here is another exercise for you to do, sometime before you move on to the next chapter. Take ten to fifteen minutes to do an inquiry. Begin by checking in to where you are, and then inquire in an open way into whatever you find, diving down by questioning and exploring more deeply.

At the end of the inquiry, take a further five minutes to look back over your inquiry and see if you can notice where the inquiry was free. What were you open to? What was fine to be there, and how did that feel? Also see if there were any moments when there was less openness and freedom, where you felt your inner critic was making you feel that you were doing it wrong or that something was wrong with what you were experiencing. If there was something that you were not so open to or that seemed wrong, look more closely and see if you can notice *what* was wrong. What was not OK? Was it that you didn't know something? Or was there a feeling that was not OK? Was it something about how you were doing, as if you are doing it wrong, or did you feel stupid because you felt lost?

And if you do not notice the inner critic, that is fine too—see if it sneaks in to start making you feel bad about that! In any case, one day you probably will recognize it in action, so there is no need to push it.

Before the next chapter, make a list of some of the things that the inner critic makes you feel are wrong or bad or should not be happening. You will use your list for the next exercise.

Question and Answer: The Freedom of Inquiry

I started feeling a lot of love and sexual desire in my inquiry the other day for all sorts of people. Surely that is not right and shouldn't be there, right? I totally agree with my inner critic on this one! If I let that happen, there is going to be all sorts of trouble.

This is definitely something to look into for yourself. You will probably find that there is something true in what your inner critic is saying: if you acted on all your desires (sexual or otherwise) and everyone did the same, the world would be a real mess. But the key thing is the difference between acting on something and experiencing it and exploring it. We will go into this further in chapter 12, but in a nutshell, remember that inquiry is not about simply acting out your experience. It is about allowing and being with your experience so that you can explore it to find out what is true in it.

There is truth to be discovered in the *what* of it: What is the desire? How do you experience it? What is the energy of it like for you? What is the part of you that gets activated? What happens when you let yourself feel it without acting it out in your life? There are very important qualities of your nature at play in there and so much richness to discover. And there is truth to be discovered in the *why* of it: How come? What is making you get so aroused and juicy? What is bringing about this response? Why this particular response? There is important meaning in there to be discovered. It is not there by accident.

The inner critic would simply put a stop to the whole thing and have you never get in touch with your desires, and never be able to penetrate them to discover the hidden secrets. The same is true of things such as aggressions and hatred, or any other experience that looks like it will make a mess if you just run with it. It is vital to remember that inquiry invites you to sense your arms and legs, look and listen, and be present with your experience whatever it might be. You do this little by little as you build the capacity to do so. And you do not simply act out everything that comes up.

And then, as a capable and responsible adult, you will get to see what you really want to do, based on what is really true for you and appropriate for your circumstances. You can discover how you want to express some aspect of yourself in your life in a truthful way with integrity.

TEN

The Magic of Inquiry

SPACE FOR THE MAGIC

So what is the magic of inquiry? What is so great about getting in touch with and clear about whatever comes up in your experience, in a totally open way? It is something that you have to give a little time to allow to happen. But the more you inquire, the more you will begin to see for yourself.

When you fully experience something—when you are totally with the feelings, thoughts, and sensations, and when you really clearly see it for what it is—something very magical happens all by itself, if you just give it a moment. The very clarification itself has an impact on you. You know this yourself, I am sure. Maybe you can think of a time when something was bothering you and you did not really understand what was going on, and when you finally got it, something in you went "Oh . . . oh my goodness, *that* is what's happening!" and the realization shifted you in a deep way.

So as you realize a bit more about your inner world, even just noticing a little more clearly what is actually around, you can always take a moment and wonder, "How is this for me?" or "How do I feel about this?" or "How does it affect me to see/experience/feel/sense this?" and see what happens.

This magic does not happen just by thinking about things. You have to be fully in touch with your experience as well. It also does not happen, for example, just by feeling a strong feeling. The real magic takes both ingredients: you need to be in touch with your experience while also recognizing it, seeing the truth more clearly. And then you give yourself a little space for the magic. "Ah, how is this . . .?" and you notice how it affects you.

So this is another kind of question that might come into your inquiry, another angle of curious, interested contemplation: "Hmm, what is that like for me? What happens as I see this?"

As with any other element of inquiry, you are interested in whatever happens to be true. You might find yourself unaffected by what you are seeing, or you might find yourself touched in some way by the truth. You might be bored by it or angry about it or sad with it. You might be loving or grateful or fortified by what you are in touch with and recognizing. It could affect you in all sorts of ways, and what matters is that you give that some space and be as curious about that as the initial experience. You are giving your experience space to affect you and change you.

You see, there is one particular way in which diving in your inner experience is different from diving in the outer ocean. The inner world is magical in a way that the outer world is not. With inquiry, you are diving into your own consciousness, and the act of doing so begins changing what is happening in your consciousness. The very act of becoming aware of something in your experience and articulating it will impact you and shift your experience in some way. Some dynamic movement begins to happen—perhaps subtle, perhaps not so subtle. Maybe you had not realized you were sad until you sat down and noticed it, and that might touch you in some way. It could be just a little pique of interest. It could be a strong aversion or concern. There may be a sense of relief at naming what you are feeling. You might notice the very waters of the inner ocean soften and you feel gentle and kind with the sadness that you are experiencing.

Whatever it is, you can notice something dynamic happening pretty much right from the beginning, as soon as you start bringing awareness and clarity to your experience. The landscape itself shifts as you explore, and that landscape is nothing other than your own consciousness and your own self. So you might begin to see that this magical property of inner experience can make for an interesting adventure!

There is a flow between looking around and finding something, sensing and feeling into that, recognizing and articulating where you are, and letting yourself be impacted by what you are finding, and then recognizing and verbalizing *that*.

MAGIC AND THE INNER CRITIC

This magic applies to any experience at all. We are going to look here at how it applies to exploring the inner critic. As we explored in the previous chapter, this inner lifeguard can create difficult feelings and a sense of being stuck if you do not know how to work with it. It can be discouraging, which is, after all, its entire aim: to discourage you from the truth! But if you have some forewarning and some tools, you might be more up for the encounter with the lifeguard when it arrives, and that encounter can be quite exhilarating! This lifeguard is guarding the gates to your freedom, and there is no way around getting down and dirty here at some point. The magic of inquiry will come to your aid!

So get in touch and get clear, and see how that affects you. How do these help with the inner critic?

The first step is to recognize when your inner critic is active. How does it show up in your inner world? We touched on this some in the previous chapter. In the body there can be a feeling of lack of energy, lifelessness, depression; a sense of feeling small and put upon, as if the whole world is on your case, making you feel inferior, bad, defeated. In the heart there can be feelings of guilt or shame; a sense of being criticized, devalued, diminished, or wrong. And in the mind you might notice a mean, attacking voice giving you a hard time; or a stream of advice, criticism, guidance, or encouragement, trying to push you one way or the other or getting on your case about this or that. "Do this, do not do that, what is wrong with you, how could you, you're so selfish, you didn't really mean that, you do not know what you're doing . . ." and so on. You might be stuck in endless debates trying to justify yourself.

The inner critic can come up around any area of your experience: what you feel, what you think, how you look, what you want, what you love, what seems to be missing, when you are feeling something good (like love) or something bad (like fear). Any element of the inner world could be the object of its attack, leaving you feeling that the experience is not OK and should not be allowed.

The hallmark of the inner critic is that it tries to push you away from whatever you are actually experiencing and make you feel small, bad, or wrong for it. As we explored in the previous chapter, the litmus test is simply to ask yourself, "Is it OK for me to be with this . . . with what I'm experiencing?" If you find that it *is* OK, even if it is difficult or unpleasant in some way, then the inner critic has not got you. If you are able to be with what is there, then there might be lots to explore, but not particularly about the inner critic. But if you feel like you really should not be allowing what is there, that you should not be having this feeling, thought, or experience, and that it is not OK, as if you were being judged, criticized, or shamed for it . . . then the inner critic is active. It has caught you in its grip!

Waking up and getting in touch with this activity when it happens is crucial. It is also not the most comfortable process. It is not easy to really let yourself feel into these feelings of shame, guilt, or diminishment; to become aware of these critical thoughts; or to sense how your body feels and how your whole inner experience gets contracted, tight, and limited. Sometimes there is a contraction and tightness in the right shoulder, neck, and head area, as if a voice up there is nagging or yelling in your ear. But it is really important to let yourself get curious about this phenomenon and feel into it. You can get curious about however this lifeguard shows up in your inquiry when it does—and all the little tricks that it uses!

As you do so, you will start getting clearer. You can wonder, "What is it actually saying? What is it pushing me away from or toward? What is it implying about me, or explicitly telling me?"

Sometimes it goes well beyond merely advising to an outright attack: "You screwed that up, now you'll never amount to anything. How could you! You're worthless!"

If you notice an inner critic attack like that, you can then begin exploring the attack. Get as clear about it as you can. What exactly is it saying or implying? Sometimes it is just a feeling rather than an explicit attack, but even then you can usually sum up that feeling into an implied message. If you feel bad about what you are experiencing, then there is the implicit message in that feeling that your experience is bad, or that you are bad, even if you do not hear words saying that.

Some people notice lots of nagging words going on and on and on. In this case, you can often distill it down to a very short sentence and say it as if it were someone else talking to you. It usually boils down to something like, "What's wrong with you!" or "You're a mess!" or "You're too big for your boots!" Often they are variations on the theme of how you are too much or too little, bad, wrong, useless, or worthless—something in that department. Get as clear as you can.

You can get even clearer. What exactly is it attacking? What exactly about you or your experience supposedly makes you bad or worthless?

You might also notice how it feels. As we saw before, it is as if there is one part of your psyche attacking another part. You might imagine your inner critic sitting across from you, in a chair opposite you, talking to you. How does it seem? Does it seem big or small? Friendly or mean? What other characteristics about it do you notice? Often you might find one of your parents or other childhood figures showing up there. So you can just be interested to see what you can see about it.

In this process, you are getting more in touch and clearer as you inquire into the attack. As you do this, notice how it affects you to be getting so clear about it. How does it make you feel to recognize this attack? How is it to recognize clearly that there is basically some voice or message telling you, in a mean way, that you are bad or useless? If you stay in touch, feeling and seeing it for what it is, how do you feel about it? Do you like it? This is a moment for the magic.

You can inquire not only into the inner critic part but also the part of you that is on the receiving end, the part you probably usually identify with. Without trying to change it, what is it like to have this attack coming at you? Often it makes you feel small, anxious, afraid, hurt, ashamed, guilty, humiliated—a whole range of unpleasant feelings. It is not easy to allow and explore these feelings. But you can inquire and see how this truly affects you.

Usually we hide from the inner critic by trying to comply with its rules. Or maybe we agree with it or debate with it, or we fight against it. But all of these are ways of getting entangled with the inner critic. You are continuing to treat it as if it were real and true rather than simply a voice from the past in your head. You either do what it says or you fight or argue with it. But by inquiring, you are stepping out of that automatic obedience and actually exploring it, being with the whole phenomenon and being interested in it. You are not just taking it at face value and running with it but rather finding out what on earth is really going on. You are letting yourself see what is happening inside you. The more clearly you see it and feel it, the more that will affect you.

And here comes the magic of inquiry. The very process of being more in touch with it and seeing the truth of it a little more clearly will all by itself have a transforming effect on your inner world. It invites the magic of your human nature, your essence, to appear as you ask yourself, "Well, how do I feel about this? How is this for me?"

I am going to mention two specific magics that can happen here.

The Magic of Kindness

The first is that as you look more into how the attack affects you, focusing on you who is being attacked rather than on the inner critic itself, you might really get in touch with how painful the attack is, how limiting and hurtful it is for you. Often this will connect you with some sense of being young and small and scared, being yelled at or bullied by some grown-up. You might see how much suffering it causes in your life. When you recognize this, you can take a moment to see how it is to feel and see this. How is it to see this part of you that is so afraid and having such a hard time? How do you feel about the difficulty that you are going through with this barrier? At some point, feeling and recognizing the suffering often brings a very natural response of kindness and care. You start to feel sorry for yourself, perhaps both now in the moment, or for that young child that you were. If you saw someone beating up on a little kid, you would probably just naturally feel sorry for them; you would want to give them a hug and make them feel better. And when you see this bullying activity going on inside you, the same response can arise for the part of you that is bullied. The very waters of your inner ocean may begin to flow with this kindness and gentleness for all the hurt, which turns out to be exactly what is needed.

Although feeling and recognizing the hurt and suffering caused by the inner critic may seem unappealing, it is exactly what will bring you to this gentle, caring kindness for yourself. This kindness is a quality of your essence, your inner human nature. It is a treasure of the inner ocean, warm and kind and caring, and infinitely responsive and attuned to your hurt and suffering. This compassionate presence helps you deal with all manner of hurt and difficulty. When you feel that kindness, the lifeguard may begin to melt in some way—it turns out it was making up for the lack of kindness in your childhood. When your inner ocean rediscovers its own gentle kindness, then you do not need the inner critic to beat you up to keep you out of trouble.

The Magic of Strength

The second magic possible here tends to come more from exploring the inner critic itself—the sense of this "other" who is attacking you. As you discover kindness toward yourself, you might start to feel angry at the one who is attacking you, at the inner critic itself—just like if you saw someone bullying a child on the playground. You would naturally go up to them and say, "Stop!" You might find you get angry, and as you let the truth of that happen, the waters of the inner ocean start to flow with fiery, strong energy. It is simply true that you do not like it, that you do not want to be spoken to like this! This fire can arise very naturally. The more you recognize the negative messages coming at you and ask, "Do I like this? How is this for me that there is a sense of someone 'else' making me feel useless and terrible," the more you might get really pissed off. That anger is the beginning of this magic: "Stop it! Get lost! Nobody gets to talk to me like that. I'm not continuing this conversation."

This is a very important step. You are sending that lifeguard packing. You are daring to confront this inner authority. You are telling it to get lost, to leave you alone and let you live your life and explore your inner ocean because it is yours and you can find out what is true for yourself. You are simply not a little kid anymore. The anger is a doorway to your fiery strength, which is another treasure of the inner ocean, a quality of your human nature. And the strength will come up to chase that inner critic right out of the water, to send it back to the beach, so that you can continue your adventure.

We call this *disengaging from the inner critic*. In time, whenever you spot an attack, whenever you notice you feel criticized for something that you are experiencing, you will begin to wonder what the judgment is; and when you see it, you will tell that lifeguard to take a hike! Your healthy aggression will come up to defend the truth of your experience.

There will be times in your process when you need to actively flex this muscle. The inner critic keeps trying to push you away from your experience, from whatever is true and actually going on for you. And at some point it has to be challenged or it will keep you limited and restricted and you will never escape the pond. As you recognize the truth of its activity, its limitation, the suffering it causes, and its redundancy, you may become more and more motivated to deal with it effectively. Sometimes that means telling it to get lost, even when you feel that you do not have what it takes. It is very important to continue the exploration to find out what stops you from challenging it and, in time, to begin to break free. If you do find yourself completely unable to challenge it, which can happen, it can be useful to look more closely again at the one who is on the receiving end of the attack, the sense of "you" who is being criticized. See if there is that young child in there, who might need a hug or some other gentle attention before the fire can come bursting out.

The liberating magic will start happening the more you feel and recognize the inner critic's activity and the truth of how it affects you, and how you feel about that. The more you clarify both sides of this dynamic—the criticized one, and the criticizer—the more it will open up and transform. Conversely, the more you avoid it, ignore it, argue with it, rebel against it, pretend it is not there, pretend it is OK, spiritualize it, or stay vague about it, the more it will remain intact and limit your freedom to murky nets and little ponds.

Learning to dive and navigate with this tricky denizen of the inner world is a lifelong process. Each time some new aspect of the inner ocean begins revealing itself, the inner critic usually gets activated and can make you feel bad, even after many years on the path. So it is good to be prepared and realistic about it. The resources section at the end of the book contains several options to help you develop your skills in more depth, and to unlock the different kinds of magic that can help you defeat it.

We have explored the magic of inquiry in detail in the context of the inner critic, because it is a structure that many people encounter early on as they begin to explore and articulate their experience. But the magic of inquiry is much, much broader than a vital aid for transforming the inner critic. The magic arises any time you bring more in-touchness and more clarity and recognition of truth to your experience. It usually arises on the frontiers of our experience, when we come to some place that is not familiar, where we would not usually go. It happens when we recognize something that we have not recognized before, perhaps have not been able to recognize before. As you hang out with yourself and let yourself feel and know and sense your experience, you may be touched by the truth of what you see in some way, and the qualities of your essence begin responding to your experience in ways that are totally unexpected, unforeseen and indeed unforeseeable. You never know where it is going or what will respond. The journey of inquiry becomes a magical transformational unfolding, occurring right where you are, without ever trying to go anywhere other than simply being with what is true for you.

EXERCISE: THE MAGIC OF INQUIRY

Here is a general exercise to explore the magic of inquiry. Begin with a few minutes of kath meditation, and transition out of the meditation by sensing, looking, and listening. Then check in and begin exploring for five minutes, simply exploring where you are and what is around for you. After five minutes, pause, and then take a few moments to contemplate how you are affected by what you are exploring. How is it to be recognizing and experiencing whatever it is you are feeling, sensing, recognizing, and understanding? Allow whatever comes up here—it might be positive or negative. Keep an eye out for the judgment of the inner critic, but also notice other responses. You might find reactions like boredom, irritation, or disappointment as you see where you are. You might get curious about those. Or you might find your true nature beginning to respond with curiosity, relaxation, clarity, kindness, aliveness, intimacy, quietness, spaciousness, or solidity—in which case you can get a little clearer about what that's like. After a few minutes, go back to the main exploration and see what happens then as you continue exploring for another five minutes. You can go back and forth between the primary exploration and giving yourself time to be affected by what you are finding.

EXERCISE: EXPLORING THE INNER CRITIC

Here is a second exercise to explore the magic of inquiry in the specific context of the inner critic. Inquire into your experience of your inner critic. Pick one of the areas where you have discovered that it gets on your case. Here are some avenues to explore. You will almost certainly not get to all of them in one fifteen-minute inquiry, but these are pointers to some of the directions that you might explore when your inner critic shows up. After each one, I also include the kind of question you might ask to invite the magic.

- See if you can identify clearly what is being attacked—your appearance, your performance, your feelings, a thought or realization, a young part of you—something true, whatever it might be. As you see this, how is it to see that you are attacked for this particular part of your experience? How do you feel about that?
- See if you can find out what the message is. What is the attack? Can you distill it down to a short, punchy sentence? Even if your inner critic is just a vague feeling, you might be able to find some implied message that conveys the meaning of the feeling. How is it to recognize the essence of the attack?
- What do you usually do with this attack? Do you try to explain your way out of it? Do you agree with it and feel bad? Do you hit back or rebel? As you recognize this, how does it affect you to see how you usually get mired with your inner critic?
- If you do not do what you usually do and just let yourself see and feel the attack, how does it affect you? How is that for you? How does it make you feel to be on the receiving end of an attack like that?
- Explore the other side of the phenomenon too: How does the inner critic itself seem to you? You might even consider letting yourself be the inner critic, to see what it feels like to be yelling and attacking in whatever voice it seems to have.

- Finally, once you have spotted it and seen some of its effects, you might try simply telling it to get lost: "Go away," "Go hang out with someone else," "Fuck off"—whatever it takes. If you feel you cannot do this, see what seems to get in the way, or see if something else is drawing you.

This illustrates how each time you feel into and recognize something new at any part of the process (not only the inner critic!), you can give yourself time to be affected by that and see how it affects you: "How is that for me? How do I feel about this?"

Between now and the next lesson, continue your practice of inquiry. Take fifteen minutes once or twice a day to explore where you are, being open to whatever you are finding, staying in touch with and exploring your experience. As you do this, each time you get in touch with something and recognize more clearly what is there, take some time to be affected by what you are seeing. How does it affect you to be in touch with and see what you are seeing? This creates an opening for the magic.

Question and Answer: The Magic of Inquiry

If we are supposed to be friendly and interested in everything in the inner ocean, why are we not open to the inner critic? I don't understand why we try to get rid of this but not anything else.

We are indeed open to everything in the inner ocean, including the inner critic. That is why we need to bring it to light and see as much about it as we can. We are also impacted by the truth of what we see. Remember, the truth is the point. So when you see that you are feeling sad, for example, and there is a voice in your psyche that is making you feel bad about having sadness, you might wonder, "What is true here?" Does this help me? Is this force supporting me to be with my truth?" In time, you will see that what is true is that the inner critic is specifically pushing you away from the truth. That is actually true. It is true that this hurts you and limits you. You can discover all facets of truth about it: the truth that it comes from your childhood, the truth that it makes you feel like a child, the truth that inside that feeling of being judged you actually feel like a child, the truth that that is only a memory or image from the past, the truth that that is no longer who you are. Going through all of this discovery is important in your inquiry, and in time it will increasingly liberate you from the inner critic.

The more you recognize these truths, the more you will also recognize the probable truth that the force of it hangs around persistently, pushing you away from your truth, and that you need to challenge its grip. So, sometimes, even though you do not fully bottom out the whole process, it is nevertheless useful simply to challenge it directly to loosen its grip so that you can be wherever it is you are.

Disengaging from the inner critic is not exactly trying to get rid of it. What you are doing is challenging the way it restricts you and pushes you away from your truth. When you tell it to get lost, you are simply challenging the habit that you learned as a child of moving away from your truth in response. Because ultimately, it is also true that it is simply a voice in your psyche.

Disengaging from the inner critic is, then, a practice. When we are deeply settled in our truth, disengaging becomes less necessary, since the inner critic cannot knock us away from what is true. But in an ongoing way—just like meditation, inquiry, sensing your arms and legs, and not acting out your experience—actively disengaging when it knocks you off course is a step along the way, a muscle to flex to support you on your journey.

When I saw all the ways my inner critic attacks me, I didn't get angry, I just thought it was totally absurd. I couldn't stop laughing at the craziness of it. Why didn't I get angry or feel compassion for myself?

There are many other magics beyond the magics of strength and kindness. When you recognize and are impacted by the truth of your experience, your being can respond in many different ways, and if it is available, it will respond with exactly the magic that is most needed in that moment. In your case, it seems the magic of lightness arose at the absurdity of the situation and that seemed to be exactly what was needed to deal with the totally pervasive heaviness of the inner critic. Wonderful! Sometimes the process might bring humility, determination, or a sense of your own value. The anger that becomes healthy aggression and the hurt that brings compassion are two important responses that have been highlighted because they are often so needed. But you can be open to however your own soul responds—there is no "should" here either!

PART THREE

The Three Centers

ELEVEN

The Head Center

KNOWING AND LEARNING

Your experience includes your circumstances, your body, your heart, and your mind. Inquiry means getting in touch with your experience, finding where you are, and then exploring what it is and what it is about in order to see what is true. It means looking deeper than the first glance at the surface. As you do, the very waters of your inner ocean itself begin responding in a magical way to what you contact and recognize.

All of this is based on a very fundamental property of your experience. It is so obvious and so fundamental that you might miss it. It is all based on your capacity to recognize and know what you are experiencing. This is the capacity of the mind, or what we call the *head center*. You will see soon why it is called the head center, though you might have noticed that intuitively, most people will point to their head when they talk about their mind.

Mind is one of the basic layers or dimensions of your psyche. The usual experience of your mind can appear as a flow of thoughts or ideas; as labeling, commentary, concepts, or associations and comparisons appearing with whatever else is going on in your experience. Mental content can also include images—for example, imaginations, or the visual snapshots or snippets of past experience that appear in some memories. Much of your conditioning and the history that shapes and influences you now appears in the form of images and memories held within your consciousness.

You look at a fish and the thought "fish" might arise, and then the various features of the fish arise as you continue looking at it. You might have opinions or assessments about its colors, your knowledge about that species of fish might come to mind, or you may remember a similar one you saw the other day. All of this is the usual mental content of experience.

At the same time, a different kind of knowing is also going on. Aside from the labels and commentary brought in from past learning, there is simply the fact that your consciousness is able to recognize a fish when it sees it, and to make out the colors and features of it. The knowing is right there, right now, as your immediate consciousness of the experience. You can look around where you are and recognize where you are and what you are seeing: you are conscious of what you see and that consciousness simultaneously includes knowing and recognizing it. When you become conscious that you feel hungry, you know that; you recognize hunger as hunger. You sense your leg and know it is your leg, and you are conscious of the details of whatever you are experiencing as you are sensing. You can feel contentment, and as you feel and are conscious of the contentment, you can recognize it as such. This is not just the snapshot of memory or the flow of inner chatter that you might usually think of as mind. Those usual experiences of mind are rather the snapshots from this broader immediate consciousness, that are stored and remembered and recalled as needed.

Your mind, your consciousness, is doing it right now, making out the words that you are reading as you are reading. This consciousness is continually operating fresh in the present moment, in the now. It is the very consciousness and recognition of your experience, and I mean this in a simple and nonesoteric way—the mere fact that you are knowing at least some of what is going on.

This immediate knowing and recognizing of experience as it is happening is central to inquiry. In the Diamond Approach, it is called *basic knowledge*. Some spiritual practices seek to bypass or drop the mind, but here we are using the mind. We can even use the mind to explore beyond mind into the places of no mind, which some of you may be familiar with.

So this immediate knowing is like looking around underwater and seeing brightly colored fish, slimy seaweed, and jagged rocks, and recognizing and discriminating that as what you are seeing. You might not yet know the name of the fish or what it does, or why that seaweed is growing between those rocks, but you can take the time to know and recognize what you are experiencing as it is happening.

This capacity is fundamental to inquiry. When you inquire into your experience, you let yourself take the time to be in touch with what is happening, and to be informed by the immediate recognition and knowing of your immediate experience as it is happening. You are in touch with and beginning to discriminate and recognize the relevant features of your situation, your thoughts and ideas, your feelings and your sensations.

Your mind has this capacity to know your experience in the moment. It also has the capacity to learn from your experience. It can accumulate that knowing, and it develops a range of all the kinds of things it is able to recognize and think about even when they are not immediately present. This is what we more often think of as mind and knowledge. So the next time you go diving and see the same brightly colored fish again, you think, "Oh, I know what that is, I've seen that before. Last time it went swimming over there, before this other fish with all these teeth popped out and ate it! And then I read up on it." You can rattle off everything you now know about it. This more ordinary type of knowledge is based on what you have learned from your immediate experience and from what you have read and picked up from people around you. This is the more conventional sense of mind, and the content of that learning—all those ideas, associations, images, and thoughts—are what many people think of as mind. And, indeed, it is an important facet of mind. But as you see, there is more to it.

Your mind has been learning through every moment that you have ever lived, taking snapshots and impressions of the immediate consciousness of your experience and extracting concepts and understanding from them. The outcome is the accumulated ideas and knowledge that you have about yourself—what you are, what you love, what you want, what you should do, how you should live. It's also about reality—what the world is, what other people are, what any particular area of living is. This capacity to learn is extraordinary. The mind does not come with knowledge about everything in the world built in! We know that certain tendencies and impulses come built into a baby. But a great deal is learned through experience. Back to our diving analogy, and every time you go diving in the sea, you add to that knowledge. You learn a bit more about the terrain, what lives there, what happens at different times of day, what kind of creatures come out when. You learn where to go if you want to see giant eels, watch the thrill of a hunt, or play with dolphins. It is all learned, and every time you dive you learn more. Diving is like this. Life is like this. And inquiry is like this too.

Learning goes beyond just knowing what is happening. Your consciousness links up what it is recognizing now with what you have learned in the past. It can recognize the patterns and connections in your experience with what you have already learned. This is what it means to *understand* your experience. Understanding happens when your mind sees things in a way that really makes sense to you, where all the pieces link up.

Understanding in inquiry is not just about having a nice theory. That is a mental understanding. Understanding in inquiry is being in the middle of what is happening and as you are in it, right there, you *get* what is going on. This gives that deep-down, aha kind of understanding: "Oh, that is what's going on here. That's what it's about. I get it! Oh, look, that's a stinging sea anemone and that little clown fish lives there because it is immune to the stings, and they kind of look after each other." You are getting all of this as you watch and discover. It is amazing!

IGNORANCE AND OBSOLESCENCE

This wonderful learning mind comes with two types of challenges though. The first is that it starts off not knowing. Your mind arrives largely ignorant, without much knowledge, precisely so that it can learn whatever it needs to from the unique experience of your life! And as you go through life, no matter how much you have already learned from the past and how much you may know, the inner ocean is vast beyond imagining. There is so much that you do not know yet! Inquiry is guaranteed to bring you somewhere you do not yet know. If you think about it, any transformation practice by definition must bring you somewhere new; otherwise you are just swimming around in circles and nothing would be transforming. Something new is, by definition, something unknown. It is as if the areas of the inner world that are unknown to you are simply veiled in darkness. There is no light there yet for you to see and know what is there. So you have to be willing to not know, to edge into the darkness and the unknown and keep exploring to bring more light. If your inner critic has a problem with not knowing, you may need to tell that lifeguard to back off and leave you be, or it will keep dragging you back into the familiar pond that you already know so well.

So the first challenge is ignorance. The second challenge of the learning mind is that often some of the older learning that was exciting and new in the past has become obsolete. Things have moved on since then! But the understandings and learnings that you picked up hang around and shape your current experience in various ways that you do not see. This is basically what conditioning is. Some of that old learning is really, really out of date. It was once true, or seemed true. It was truth that you were able to make out when you were a child! But much of it is definitely not true anymore.

The inner critic is a great example of this kind of obsolescence. Sure, it was very important when you were a child to learn your parents' rules and be obedient in order to stay out of trouble. But now? Do you still need to feel guilty and be yelled at if you are a few minutes late? Is it really true that you should never feel sad? Is it actually the case that it is not OK to sit back and relax for once?

Old learning also shows up when you just think you know. The minute you go, "OK, I know what that is," the exploration is over. It shuts down right there: "Yes, that sensation is just my stomach.

That's what it is and there's nothing else to find out about it." "That feeling is sadness. I know what that is. There's nothing more to see." So while it might be true that you know *something* about the experience, it is also true that if you stay with the experience in an open and curious way, more will emerge. Every single experience in the inner world—every single experience—contains more to discover. You never, ever know something definitively. The inner world is far more mysterious and fascinating than that. You can approach what seems like a completely familiar feeling, thought, or reaction, and if you don't assume you know everything about it and you approach it with not knowing, with openness, you will undoubtedly discover something new. So you need to learn to hold your knowledge lightly, in a way that does not block the openness to find out more.

All this old learning and out-of-date learning is like the murk, muck, and dirt floating in the water of the inner world. You are swimming around and you can barely see more than a foot in front of your nose because your history and all the old ideas from your past obscure your view. You think there is nothing more to see when actually there is an entire magnificent world that you are missing. The water of the inner world is polluted, blocked, cloudy, and sometimes downright toxic.

The combination of past learning and ignorance leads to some challenging barriers that can halt the unfolding of the inquiry. What to do? Well, the same thing we always do. Just get in touch with and get as clear as you can about what is happening. In this case, that means checking out what ideas, beliefs, assumptions, and associations you might have about your experience and trying to catch yourself when you are assuming that you know definitively what something is.

You can ask yourself, "What do I make of this? What do I think I know about this? What ideas do I have about this?" You need to see these assumptions and beliefs, and when you do, the magic of inquiry can begin to bring more clarity.

The aim of seeing these assumptions and beliefs is not to get rid of them. It is simply to be in touch with them and to be clear about, to understand, what is going on. As you become aware of your assumptions, you will see for yourself how they close down your exploration. You will also see where you back away from not knowing. The more you see these, the more willing you may become to stay open and curious. The magic of inquiry will continue acting!

If you find you do not know something, you might grow to embrace that and get really interested: "Wow—I've come to the edge of what I know! I'm entering into something really new! What could be going on here?!"

EXERCISE:
EXPLORING OLD AND NEW KNOWLEDGE

Check in and explore what is around in your inner world, be it some situation or certain feelings, sensations, and thoughts. Just look at whatever is up for you in an open, friendly, and interested way, letting yourself notice and be in touch with what's present. Do this for about five to ten minutes.

Then spend a few minutes asking yourself, "What do I think I know about this?" or "What ideas do I have about this?" to see what ideas you have about your experience. Ask the question several times and just see what answers pop out of your mouth or onto your page.

After that, spend a few minutes contemplating "What do I *not* fully know or understand about this?" to see some areas that you do not yet know or understand in the experience. Again, just answer spontaneously whatever comes to mind.

Then spend a few minutes contemplating "What can I recognize and tell from the immediate experience right here and now?" so you take a few minutes to see what immediate new knowing and recognition of your experience is happening right there. Do this in a relaxed and easy way as you simply contemplate your experience to see what you can tell from it.

You could repeat this exercise in some form between now and the next lesson. Take the usual ten to fifteen minutes each day to inquire into your experience. Afterward, take some time to look at what you think you know about it, what you do not know, and what you recognize and understand freshly.

Question and Answer: The Head Center

My mind has gone totally blank! Now what?!

How interesting! What happens if you just stay with it, hang out with that experience, having no thoughts, just a kind of blankness? See what sensations you notice as you sense your forehead or the top of your head. Just hang out with the experience in a curious and friendly way, allowing whatever feelings come up, and see what happens. If fears come up, check out the fears. You might find you are afraid of not being able to think again, or not being able to function. But probably if you give it a little time you will still be able to lift your arm, and talk, even if there are no thoughts in your mind. It can be a fascinating discovery! See what else you can notice about the blankness itself. What kind of blankness is it? Empty? Clear, like air? Or dark, like the night sky? Simply continue exploring...

My mind never shuts up! There's a voice chattering away the whole time, no matter how hard I try to let it go.

What if you don't try to let it go and instead get curious and interested in it? What is this part of your mind that is chattering? What is it saying? What is it chattering about? Is it a conversation? If so, between what parts? As you draw closer to the chattering, see what feelings you notice at the same time. Often when you are only aware of intense mental activity, there is an emotional and felt sense going on underneath that is beneath awareness, so you could get curious about that. How is this chattering part of you feeling? And what sensations do you find in your body?

I've learned to let go of my mind and my ideas since they are not real. Surely it will not be helpful to focus on them more, right?

You might be able to let go of your ideas and thoughts for a few moments here and there, but ultimately bringing them into consciousness and seeing them for what they are and discovering how they are truly impacting you is a very powerful tool for transforming the mind. We have all sorts of ideas and beliefs that are definitely not true and definitely not real. They nonetheless very powerfully shape our experience of reality in deep and persistent ways. In inquiry, we do not attempt to get rid of them or change them. We simply bring them to light to see them for what they are. Sometimes this means that you will feel the weight of your beliefs and ideas clogging up your consciousness even more fully, but that is a step along the way toward truly transforming them. Then you will not need to keep telling yourself that they are not real and stepping away from them or dropping them, which is an act of manipulating your experience in some way. With inquiry, you rather bring them to light and discover the parts of you that think these things are true. In time, you will simply know them for what they are and your experience will change all by itself in a more natural way.

TWELVE

The Heart Center

THE WORLD OF FEELINGS

One of the dimensions of your experience that you might have a whole lot of old knowledge and out-of-date ideas about is the realm of your heart, the realm of feelings. It is to this realm that we will turn next.

When I say "heart," I simply mean the whole range of your feelings, and we will see more clearly over the final chapters why it is called the *heart center*. It is not really referring to the physical organ in your chest that pumps your blood, but it does refer to something that you might feel experientially in the center of your chest.

Heart is really what makes all experience feel meaningful and gives it richness and feeling. Heart means happiness, joy, pleasure, satisfaction, fulfillment, love, kindness, value, richness, purity, humanness, friendliness, passion, courage, significance, meaningfulness. The *feeling* sense of all the qualities of our nature is experienced through the heart. Our heart is often the center of what we experience as our humanity. Without heart—without kindness, love, joy, and feelings of all kinds—we do not feel truly human. Your heart is your very capacity to feel and to be touched emotionally, affectively.

Heart also involves the entire range of emotional reactions—anger, sadness, hurt, frustration, envy, jealousy, greed, and so on. These are all feelings that arise in the heart in reaction to our situations, and more deeply in reaction to the loss of connection with our essence, our beingness.

HOLDING VERSUS ACTING OUT

When you inquire, you are pressing pause on the action of your life so that you can explore what is coming up for you, clarify what is going on, and look deeper into what is true. In terms of an external circumstance, this means allowing yourself to begin seeing the details of the circumstance and then exploring where it is you are coming from within yourself in meeting that circumstance. So you stop being busy for a bit, you stop swimming around at the surface and engaging with the circumstances. And you start diving down, diving *in*, to see the thoughts, emotions, and bodily sensations that are at play; and then you dive deeper into the qualities of your being, your presence itself.

Pressing pause on the action is especially important when it comes to feelings because feelings are the very energy and force that drive you to do things. Your mind might tell you *what* to do, but the motivation and the juice comes from your heart: your longings and desires, your loves and hates. Your inner critic lifeguard probably has very firm ideas about how these feelings need to be controlled, based on how you needed to control them when you were younger in order to fit in with your parents and your environment. You might find yourself reluctant to get in touch with your feelings in general or with specific kinds of feelings. You might have lots of ideas and old knowledge about feelings! You might think that some feelings will be dangerous or too much, or that there is simply no point in going there, all depending on your past. All of this old knowledge needs to be looked into and clarified. If you cannot go there, it will be hard to discover what is true in your feelings.

Many of these concerns come down to a deeply rooted idea that if you *feel* it, you will have to *act* on it. This is how it is for a young child: they have an emotion or feeling and immediately express it and act on it. In adults, this is what we call *acting out*. You will need to discover that this is not true for an adult. We need to be very clear here: simply taking your feelings at face value and running with them by acting out in your life is not inquiry. Inquiry means stopping, giving yourself time to get in touch, to feel and then to explore and understand your feelings and find out what is true. Some examples might illustrate this difference.

- If you feel you do not like someone, you could take it at face value that your dislike is what it is, and then you might simply avoid them, which will help you avoid ever having to feel the dislike itself. This is acting it out. It is different from going, "OK, I do not like that person. They bring up a feeling of dislike. I'm really curious about that! How interesting that I can like some people and dislike others. What does that feel like, to really feel dislike? What is going on in my consciousness there? Let me explore more deeply into that and find out about it. And also . . . what is it about? How come I dislike them so much? What is it about that specific person? If they are as they are, what is it exactly that happens in me and why? How does this affect me?" Remember, these are not questions for quick intellectual answers; each question is a whole contemplation that can reveal more in your inner world. So, you can approach the feeling of dislike with curious, interested contemplation, not getting rid of it but not simply running with it.

- If you feel kindness, you might imagine that you are going to have to rescue the whole world in some way and give away everything that you own to a charity that has your heart. Some people feel that! That is different from going, "Hmm, what is this kindness? How is it to feel that? How does it affect me? What does it make me want to do? What happens when I allow it and feel more deeply into it?" So, you are not immediately just running off with the feeling. You are taking time to explore it more fully. As it clarifies, you might decide that there is something you want to do, but it is informed by your maturity and the truth, not by a compulsive feeling.

- If the thought of doing something makes you feel guilty, and your inner critic says you should not do that, you could just never do it. In this way, you always avoid the action and you avoid the experience of being judged and feeling guilty. Here, you are being run by it, basically acting out your inner critic. Another kind of acting out would be if you are feeling terribly guilty about something that has already happened, and you run with the guilt and beat yourself up and punish yourself and grovel to everyone for weeks, months, or years. This is different from stopping and wondering, "Hmm, what's really going on here? Why do I feel so guilty? What is this feeling of guilt? Does the situation really warrant this kind of beating up on myself? If I saw someone else had done this, would I treat them in the same way? I wonder if my inner critic is at play here?"

Simply running with your feelings as they first show up can create quite a mess in your life—for you and for other people. It is basically behaving like a child. On the other hand, squashing or denying your feelings is equally unhelpful, since then you lose touch with that whole realm of your inner world, sapping away much that makes life worth living. An adult, and especially an explorer of the inner ocean, needs to learn how to *hold* the feelings. Holding a feeling means you allow it. You do not squash or suppress it. You do not just act on it. You get in touch with it as part of your freedom with your inner ocean, so that you can explore it and clarify what is true, and so that the transformational magic of inquiry can happen.

To be clear, this does not mean you *never* act on your feelings. In time, as your feelings become more and more open and clarified, they do lead to spontaneous action and expression. But at the beginning, when we are learning to inquire, we first give ourselves the time to explore: we press pause and go diving. Maybe you will do something about it later on, when you are back at the surface. Maybe not. As an adult, you will get to choose, based on what seems appropriate for your life. But knee-jerk reactions based on strong, compulsive feelings are not the actions of an adult.

Letting the feelings in might sometimes feel like letting glorious schools of sparkling technicolor fish come swimming into your world, and sometimes like coming across a depressed dolphin or a rampaging shark. It is natural to have concerns about this, and we have some tips at the end of the chapter for how to go diving safely. But the dolphin and the shark are majestic and magnificent animals that have their natural place in your inner world, if you take the time to explore and let the magic happen. You may discover that part of why they are depressed or rampaging is because the lifeguard has been keeping them caged up. Or because they have been lost in the murk and trapped in the nets of your old ideas and ignorance. Or because some magical property of the inner ocean itself—kindness, strength, or joy, for example—is needed to set them free.

You practice with feelings the same way as with everything: get more in touch with them and explore with openness and curiosity to feel them and understand them more clearly. You hang out with that attitude of "Hmm . . . interesting . . . what is this? What's happening here and how come?"

DISCRIMINATING FEELINGS

At any point in your inquiry, you can always check in with your feelings: "How am I feeling now?" Here is the first important point. *Take your time* to stay with it. Some people are not used to tuning in to their feelings, and in this case, it will take time and practice. Other people can quickly and easily feel their feelings, though even if you can recognize a feeling quickly, that is different from giving yourself time to feel and be impacted by it. You might find you are not sure what you are feeling or how you feel about something. And even when you are feeling something, it might take time to actually recognize *what* you are feeling, to find the words for it. All this is perfect—you just work with where you are.

A big part of discovering the "what" of the experience is taking time to discriminate what it is more fully. With feelings, you might start off with the basic discrimination of whether you are feeling good, neutral, or bad in some way. That is often a first level of clarifying. Then you might notice how intense it is. Is this a little school of tiny, translucent fish gently floating around or is it a powerful beast surging through the water?

Stay with it. Many people say "I feel OK" and stop there, probably slightly relieved that they are not feeling bad! "Yup, I'm fine!" But there is so much more to discover. Continue being curious and contemplating it. What exactly is this creature that is appearing? If it feels good, well, what kind of good? Is it happy good, content good, peaceful good . . .? There are so many kinds of good feelings! And if it is not good, what kind of not-good is it? Is it frustrated or sad or fearful? And so on. The recognition of the feeling comes from your contact with and curiosity about the feeling itself. Maybe the first word does not quite get it, and that is great—it means you can tell that you have not quite got it yet. Hang out, take as long as you like, and keep trying until maybe you find a word or combination of words that seems to express it well enough for you. Remember to let yourself not know and take time to find out and experiment.

This highlights the importance of staying with something in inquiry. This goes not only for feelings but for anything. The inner world takes time to reveal its riches. You need to hang out, be patient, and stay interested to see beyond the first glance. Bit by bit, the experience will reveal more and your capacity to feel and recognize more will develop.

This can go much further. You might recognize the feeling is love of some kind. Well, what kind of love? Is it gentle, sweet, appreciative love? Fiery, passionate love? Kind, warm love? Each of these qualities of love has a different feeling to it and a different meaning. The same with reactions. Is it a towering rage or a little scratchy irritation? A cold fury or an explosive outburst? The more you hang out with the feeling and explore *what* it is, the more clearly you will see and feel it for what it is.

Let's take some time to practice before moving to the next section. Take ten to fifteen minutes to explore where you are now, what's up for you, paying particular attention to the feelings that are present. Practice staying with your feelings, taking lots of time to hang out and notice more about them. Explore what they are, how they affect you.

GOING FURTHER WITH FEELINGS

A further way to explore a feeling is to use your inquiry space as a safe place in which to consciously express the feeling. This is very different from acting it out unconsciously or compulsively in your life or with somebody else. Here you are letting yourself intentionally and deliberately explore the feeling and its effects in a safe way.

You might explore how this feeling wants to be expressed. If you feel despairing or exhausted and like giving up, you might allow yourself to crumple, to just stop, or to collapse. You let that happen, all the while staying curious about how that is. If you feel excited and crazy about something—as if you wanted to rush out and go on a wild shopping spree—you could let yourself feel into that urge and run around grabbing things just to feel what that is like, to get more in touch with what is happening inside you with that feeling. If you feel angry, like you want to hit or yell at someone, you could try shouting out loud, imagining they were there, or hitting a pillow. If you feel like having someone close to you and receiving a hug, you might try taking a big pillow and giving it a hug.

The point is that you *allow* the feeling. It is not about dramatizing or overdoing the feeling but allowing it expression in a way that feels like it fits. You let yourself go there and have the feeling. You take the space to express it in a safe way and explore what the effect is, what it is trying to do *within* you. The feeling is expressing something going on *inside* you. It has an intrapsychic effect, if you allow it. This is what you can be very curious about. And it does not require you to take any external action in your life at all. You will almost certainly find that your feelings will change as you begin to give them space for exploration. And later on, you can decide what you actually need to do in your life. You might find you do not need to yell at the person after all, but feeling your inner strength and saying a few words will actually do what is needed much more effectively. But on the way to getting there, it may have been very helpful to yell in the friendly privacy of your inquiry space. Maybe you do not need to go on a huge shopping spree, but feeling your inner freedom and joy is really the answer, and then a little something that actually does fit into your budget seems just what you want and can do.

As you begin to see more of *what* the feeling is, you may begin to wonder, "How come? What is it about? Does this feeling relate to something going on in my life? Or something right here in my inner world?" Sometimes that is very obvious, and sometimes less so.

Even when the situation is obvious, it is worth not taking the feeling at face value. OK, so you feel bored at work. It might be obvious to anyone why you are bored. But if you do not stop there, and you keep exploring the feeling, well, how come? "What is the boredom, and of all the ways I could feel, why this?" After all, you could simply feel peaceful or content or simply present. But instead you feel bored. So that means something interesting is going on there. The more you are willing to explore the boredom without assuming it is a problem, without trying to pretend that it is not there, the more it can lead you somewhere new in your inner world.

Feelings are often layered on top of one another, and it takes time and exploration to follow them deeper. Each feeling turns out to be related to the feeling beneath it. So there might be a feeling of boredom. If you explore the boredom, you might find some kind of frustration underneath it, and you would see that the boredom is a reaction to cover over the frustration. Then you can get curious about that. And as you explore the frustration, it might reveal some emptiness or lack of satisfaction. You are frustrated because it feels like there is no juice, no satisfaction. Well, that makes sense of the frustration! And then you can get curious about this lack, this emptiness. Exploring this lack will take you through all sorts of history and, in time, it will be the doorway to discovering a new quality of the inner ocean itself, as the very waters begin to flow like rich, juicy, satisfying nectars. You realize the satisfaction is not about the circumstances but is intrinsic to your being. And when you discover that, you realize you are no longer bored. Life feels juicy and satisfying, even when you are just going about your mundane work.

DIVING SAFELY

A final few points about safety. There are risks to diving in the real ocean. You might stumble across a giant octopus that you do not know how to deal with, or get swept away by a wild current. There are appropriate precautions to deal with all these risks. You do not dive alone; you have a buddy who has got your back and you have theirs. You do not dive beyond your skill level. You do appropriate training for a certain number of hours in the water before venturing into deeper waters. You respect your limits.

Inquiring in the inner ocean is the same. It is an invitation to perhaps the most personal, intimate, wonderful, and incredible adventure. And it is not a party trick. In time, inquiry will take you to the heights and the depths, the heavens and the hells, the whole range of your inner world with all its feelings, as you simply explore what is true for you. With appropriate guidance and practice, you can learn to navigate all of it. This is the ultimate freedom. But you need to go gently in learning how to be with and explore intense feelings.

So here are some safety suggestions:

- Sense your arms and legs! Grounding your experience in your body is the most important way to develop your capacity to be with a wide range of feelings. If something feels intense, check in: "Can I feel my arms and legs?" Take a few minutes to really get in touch with your body. This is vital.

- If you encounter something that feels too far beyond your comfort zone, then do not push yourself. You can always say, "OK, that's enough for now. I need to stop for a bit." Climb back on the boat and take another dive tomorrow.

- Draw on the support of a diving partner, an inquiry friend. The simple presence of another person who is not inside the currents of your inner world is a great support as you explore. They can simply be present with you, sensing their arms and legs and silently witnessing your exploration. And you could do the same for them.

- Do not overdo it. Stick to relatively well-defined periods of practice—ten to twenty minutes—as you learn how to remain present with different feelings and experiences. Like developing any skill, slow and steady gradually develops the muscles to swim deeper and further with ease.

- Master divers of consciousness are available to help too. A Diamond Approach teacher can help you in your inquiry, either in person or online through Skype or Zoom or simply a phone call. Before they even start teaching, Diamond Approach teachers have at least fifteen to twenty years of doing their own inner diving and at least seven to ten years of training to guide others. They are familiar with a vast array of inner experience, and they know how to explore and navigate it skillfully. See the resources section at the end of the book for more information on Diamond Approach resources.

- Join the Diamond Net through Diamond Approach Online. The Diamond Net offers various online resources from the Ridhwan School to support you in learning how to inquire and in navigating the territory that you encounter, even if you do not have access to a group or teacher nearby.

- Join a Diamond Approach group. If this is available to you, it will be a powerful way to turbocharge your inquiry. In Diamond Approach groups, we progressively explore different elements of inner terrain over many years, in a way that seems to fit how the journey unfolds for many people.

EXERCISE: THE HEART

Take ten to fifteen minutes to explore where you are now, what is up for you, paying particular attention to the feelings that are present. This time, practice staying with your feelings, taking plenty of time to hang out and notice more about them, discriminating them more fully and finding the words that might fit to describe them. Take the time to be curious about why this feeling is here, in addition to the circumstances. Can you see anything further in your inner world that might be giving rise to it or underlying it? And you might also explore how it is to allow the feeling to be expressed in some way. This could be in very subtle ways, such as just feeling how your body softens or tightens with this particular feeling, or it could be in bigger actions, such as hugging or hitting a pillow or saying whatever the feeling makes you want to say in the tone that seems to match it. You can do anything that will not hurt or damage you or your environment. Notice the effect this has on you. Often it is useful to just hang with a feeling and take some gentle breaths to "breathe into it."

Question and Answer: The Heart

I can't really feel anything. Is something wrong?

You could find yourself unable to feel anything for a couple of reasons. One possibility is that you are simply not used to being in touch with your feelings. In this case, take plenty of time to hang out and see if you can notice something that you feel. If this seems difficult and you cannot seem to contact much, you might find a time when there are some more obvious sorts of emotion going on—for example, when something has made you laugh or cry; when you're upset, worked up, or agitated in some way; or when someone has given you a hug and you are feeling good. When you notice that happening, take some time to tune in to yourself and your feelings and see if you can notice the feeling that comes with the laughter, hug, upset, or irritation.

If, on the other hand, you *are* usually able to be in touch with your feelings and now you can't feel anything, then you might be curious to let yourself simply be with the absence of feeling. What if you don't try to make up a feeling or have a feeling but just feel the absence? See how that is and be curious about it. How do you experience it? Is it negative, neutral, or even nice in some way that there is no feeling? Most people typically refer to strong emotional reactions when they talk about their feelings, but as you become more refined in the experience of your heart, you will definitely find times when those loud feelings are not there and instead there may be something more subtle. That might be unusual at first, or unfamiliar. But as you let yourself hang out with it, gently inquiring and getting acquainted with this new way of experiencing your heart, a whole new realm may begin to open up to you.

I get overwhelmed by certain feelings—how can I learn to inquire into them?

If a feeling is overwhelming, part of what is helpful is to allow yourself to go into it slowly. Sensing your arms and your legs is a crucial container. So if it is strong, sense your arms and legs, then go into the feeling a bit. When it feels too much, come back to sensing your arms and legs, and then when you feel ready, include the feeling again. Little by little you can build your capacity to be with the feelings.

I have trauma that comes up and I need to regulate it. How can I inquire with this?

Dealing with trauma is a whole specialized field. But from a certain point of view, trauma experience is just like any other experience. Ultimately, we inquire into it to explore what is there and allow it to open up and reveal its truth. What tends to make inquiry into trauma experience so challenging is that it tends to be overwhelming and comes up unbidden. In this regard, we treat it just like any other overwhelming experience, slowly building the container of presence that will allow us to go there by sensing our arms and legs. Second, it can benefit from specialized external holding to allow it to emerge—and this is what trauma therapy can provide. Inquiry is certainly not to be confused with trauma therapy—it is not that! So if you are dealing with a trauma, you might also want to seek help with a trained professional.

The therapeutic angle tends to help people identify when difficult feelings are being activated and how to manage them and their external circumstances in relation to those feelings. This is a useful skill to develop. And at some point, it is also useful to be able to go into whatever the difficult inner experience is and to explore it when there is enough presence to be *with* it. At that point, it is may be less useful to talk about it as "my trauma," which can create a kind of distance, but rather to focus on the immediacy of the feelings and the inner experience. For example, it is more immediate to say, "I'm feeling a sense of frustration and agitation," than to say, "My trauma is being activated."

It is also worth noting that all personality structures have many sorts of wounding and difficulties within them that, in time, will surface with inquiry. This is completely normal and part of the path. The orientation of inquiry is always to be curious, friendly, and interested in a gentle and kind way, so that these difficult places can emerge and, in time, relax to reveal their inner truths. The truth is that some of them take a very long time to open up and unwind, and it takes patience and gentleness to allow this.

Finally, remember the importance of not knowing. Encapsulating an element of your experience as "trauma" can fix it in a certain way and lead you to assume you already know what it is. Indeed you do not, or not fully. So as much as possible, see if you can approach it with curiosity and immediacy.

I am feeling so good! Can I go home now?

Wonderful! It is wonderful to be feeling good, particularly if you have been feeling lousy for a while. Feeling good means that you are getting closer to feeling your true nature, because your true nature does indeed feel good. So it is great to pause here and enjoy the relief of the "problem" being gone. How is that for you? What happens in your body and your mind when you are finally feeling good? That is one angle to explore. And then . . . how about getting interested and curious in the good feeling itself? What kind of good are you feeling? Is it just the absence of anything bad? Or is it positive in some distinct way? What if you really let yourself "taste" that good feeling and identify it more clearly? This will help you integrate it more fully and even feel and enjoy it more completely!

THIRTEEN

The Belly Center

SENSATION AND GROUNDING

Thoughts and feelings, or mind and heart, are the more obvious elements of the inner world for many people. In this final chapter, we are going to focus on an element that is often far less conscious and that generally receives far less attention. Surprisingly, it will turn out to be perhaps the most important element for diamond inquiry. We are going to focus on sensations, which we usually call the *belly center*, or the body.

Sensations form the vital ground of inquiry. Sensing your arms and legs immerses you in the palpable immediacy of your felt sense, the consciousness that is actually conscious now.

Your mind can spin around in ideas, theories, and conversations that are nothing more than froth blowing on top of the water, quite divorced from the living reality below. You might think you feel this, or think that it means that, or maybe it was caused by such and such, but all of this is just guesswork and theorizing. And that, I am afraid, is not inquiry.

The same is true of the heart in some way. The heart can churn around with all sorts of emotional reactions, getting in turn upset, frustrated, delighted, excited, bored, angry, hurt, or hopeful with ourselves and our situations. The waves can be whipped up into a frenzy that also has little bearing on what is actually going on beneath the surface.

What is needed is the immediate grounding in, and contact with, your actual experience—with what is really going on. This is what the body and the belly provide. Indeed, this will finally answer the question that you might have been sitting with—of why exactly we call the head center the head center or the heart center the heart center. It is based on the immediate felt reality of our sensate experience. Just as I do not mean the physical organ when I refer to the heart or the skull and brain when I refer to the head center, I do not mean the stomach or intestines when I refer to the belly center. The centers refer to layers or dimensions of experience. In this case, it is the layer of felt sensation. Sensation is the texture of experience—the sensed, felt, immediate reality of what is present.

SENSATIONS OF THE BODY

Sensation can be explored on two levels as a start. The most common level is to explore the ordinary sensations of the body. You have practiced this by sensing your arms and legs. You might also have noticed that there are all sorts of sensations to be found in the core of your body—your pelvis, belly, chest, neck, and head. These are sometimes more intense and complex sensations. The arms and legs tend to be comparatively simple, so they are an easier place to find ground.

We have already looked at the heart and the realm of feelings. As it turns out, any feeling that you have also manifests in some kind of bodily sensation. It might be tension or movement, heat or cold. There is often an expression on your face that you might sense. You might hunch your shoulders or get tense in your neck. Your body might soften and open in an embrace or a hug. You might clench your fists or grit your teeth with certain feelings. Kindness might bring warmth. Anger might bring heat. Fear often brings coldness. Every feeling that you have also has these kinds of associated bodily sensations that you can tune in to.

Developing your sensitivity to the sensations of your body is essential for inquiry. It helps you get much more precise and clearer about what is going on. In some ways, the sensation never lies. The mind can spin, the heart can churn, but the body really tells you what is there.

THE FELT SENSE OF EXPERIENCE

Sensing the body is also the doorway to something even more significant. We call it the *felt sense*, or the *phenomenology*, of the experience. This may sound mysterious, but in fact the felt sense is far more everyday than you might think. It is evident in so many familiar English expressions.

The Sensations of the Heart Center

If someone is generous, kind, or loving, we might say they are "warm- or openhearted." Have you ever wondered why that is? If you pay attention to the sensation of your chest when you feel openhearted, you might notice that you really can sense something there—a sensation of openness, expansiveness, perhaps lovingness or joyfulness, and a sense of warmth. It turns out it is not just a metaphor: if you sense your chest area, you actually can notice it. The reason that the heart center is called the heart center is that you can often sense actual sensations related to many "heart" feelings in the chest area. When people are joyful, we might say they are "lighthearted." When they are down, we say they are "heavyhearted." Again, these are not just metaphors: in the chest you might notice sensations of bubbling lightness, or warmth or heaviness. The more you pay attention to these sensations, the more your awareness of them can grow.

The Sensations of the Head Center

The same applies with the mind and the head center. When someone has fixed ideas, we might say they are "hardheaded" or "thick-skulled." Now, their skull is not actually harder than anyone else's. But when you have fixed or rigid ideas, you can sometimes sense that your head feels hard. It might feel like you have an iron cap or helmet on your head or a leather strap tight around your brow. In contrast, your head can feel very open and spacious when you are more openminded. So these sensations are not exactly your body as you usually think of your body in a medical or anatomical kind of model, but they are sensed through your body. They are your *experience* of your body (rather than your actual physical body itself).

We say that something very intelligent is brilliant—a brilliant design, a brilliant solution, or a brilliantly executed plan. We say that a very intelligent person is bright; they are often depicted in cartoons with a light bulb drawn over their head when they have a bright idea. Again, you might notice some days that you can sense the brightness. When you feel bright, it is literally as if there is a brightness in your head, as if the lights are on. Other days you might feel dim and slow, as if your mind is sluggish and thick. So all of these qualities of mind can be sensed as immediate, palpable, felt sensations in the experience of the head itself. The mind is often called the "head center" for this very reason.

I'm just giving a couple of examples here—there are countless more.

The Sensations of the Belly Center

When you go into a situation at work, say, and you have really done all your preparation, you feel confident and solid, sturdy and grounded. You feel like you cannot be knocked off course. This is when you are anchored and at ease with reality. This is a belly-center quality of will or support, and it is often sensed in the belly and the lower body. Your legs feel solid and grounded, connected with the earth. In contrast, when you are less prepared, you might feel shaky. We often say that someone is on "shaky ground" when reality might catch them by surprise or when they are not solidly aligned with what is real. The lack of grounding can be felt in the immediate sensations of butterflies in your tummy, wobbly legs, or even having no legs or contact with the ground at all, as if you're suspended in space.

In all the instances I have mentioned—there are countless others—for all three centers, the way we commonly speak about our experience points to something that is usually on the fringe of our conscious awareness. It is not a metaphor, an idea, or a theory. It is not only a nice turn of phrase. The felt sense is something that you can tangibly notice and sense. It is the immediate texture, substance, luminosity, and color of our conscious experience, of our inner state.

You can get in touch with this by tuning in to your body more and more, and as you do, noticing what the experience is like *qualitatively*. You do this just as you did when beginning to notice more about feelings, taking your time to hang out with the sensations and see what else you notice. Do you feel heavy, thick, dense, or solid? Perhaps light, empty, buoyant, or weightless? Do you feel energized and buzzing or dull and lifeless? Full or empty? Bubbling up and overflowing or sinking down? Motionless, or tranquil, or still, or stuck, or stagnant? They are all different sensations with different corresponding feelings.

You might even notice different colors associated with sensations. You can often just start with something simple, such as noticing if a sensation seems light or dark. In time, you might notice specific colors along with different textures, such as sensing rubber or metal; water or mist; lava or roots. One day you might even discover a sensation that feels very hard and clear and sharply precise—just like a diamond.

All this might sound fanciful. You do not have to believe me, but it will be very helpful if you can at least be open to the possibility. For the inquiry, all I am inviting you to do is to consider that these sensations are actually something real in your experience, that you can tune in to them. Little by little, doing so will give you the clearest, most grounded connection with your actual inner condition. Some people find this relatively easily and for others, it takes years—there is no right or wrong here.

As you tune in to this layer of experience, swimming in the inner world takes on a whole new dimension. You begin to see that your inner world is not just intangible thoughts and feelings that *might* be this, that, or the next thing. The inner world really is a world that you can taste, touch, see, and even smell and hear. It is as palpable and real as swimming in the sea—touching the rocks or feeling the ripple of an eel; the living, pulsating, colorful mass of a coral reef; the warm, gentle holding of the water current. The wonders of the inner world are there to be explored in vivid 3D, ultra HD, as extraordinary as any underwater scene, as any fantasy or science-fictional world. Indeed, many fantasy worlds are based in some way on glimpses into the inner world. But you do not have to be happy with mere glimpses: you can journey there yourself. You can live from there every day.

These sensate experiences are immediate, tangible, palpable. They are really present. At some point you may recognize that they are *presence* itself. These are the very qualities of your consciousness appearing directly within your experience. So when you feel joy, you can sense the presence of joy welling up as a wonderful, light delightedness in your chest. You might sense in your chest a fresh lemony-yellow nectar that is pure wonder, that makes you feel so light, free, and weightless that you might just float away. It becomes clear that the joy is not just being caused by something out there but is the very presence of your own be-ingness. This exquisite yellow nectar feels like the very essence of joy, as if you distilled joy down to pure living atoms or molecules of the joy itself.

At the beginning, all you need to focus on is exploring your sensate experience together with the thoughts and feelings that are arising. The same is true of every experience, positive or negative, open or stuck. You can ground it in the sensations as you explore the feelings and thoughts, and as you do, the whole composite experience—feelings, sensations, beliefs, and ideas—begins to open up and reveal more of its truth.

When there is a feeling, you can look for the sensation. When you feel sad, what do you notice in your body? When you feel joy, what do you sense in your body? Take lots of time and be as relaxed in the exploration and contemplation as you can be. Allow and stay with the feeling of joy, and wonder, "Hmm, what am I sensing in this part of my body?" It is very helpful to breathe as you do this. Take some slightly deeper-than-normal breaths into your belly and chest and let it out through your mouth. Continue breathing, sensing, and seeing what you discover as you stay with yourself in a relaxed but alert way. There is no rush and no pressure! You might go through a kind of checklist to get started: Would you say the experience feels heavy or light? Or maybe open or closed? Do you sense more your chest or belly or head, or arms or legs? Do you notice if it's light or dark? Moving or still? And once you begin to notice something that you're curious about, stay with it and let it reveal more. Like anything, the more you practice, the more you will notice.

Many people worry at first that they are making it up, and you know, that is probably the same with any subtle perception. It's a bit like wine, coffee, or chocolate tasting—at first you can barely tell red wine from white, or one kind of coffee from another. But as you keep on tasting and exploring, you begin to notice the subtle differences. In time, you begin to sense a wider and wider range of tastes and flavors. Similarly, your inner world will emerge with greater and greater clarity and precision as you learn to trust your perceptions and take your time to sense. It will be an indispensable aid for your inquiry.

We have saved the felt sense for last because it is perhaps the least familiar sense, but in fact it is the most important. Whenever you are inquiring, it is worth taking the time periodically to check in with all three centers: What is happening in your mind? And you might also notice the sensations of your head while you do that. How are you feeling and what is happening in your heart? And you could sense your chest area as you do that. How are you landing in the reality of your overall experience—how solid are you feeling? And you can sense your belly as you do that.

EXERCISE: THE FELT SENSE

Take ten to fifteen minutes to explore where you are now, whatever is up for you, paying particular attention to the felt sense. As you explore in terms of thoughts, feelings, or circumstances, practice taking time to tune in to and notice what you sense in your body. Where is your attention drawn to as you are feeling whatever you are feeling or seeing whatever you are seeing? If nothing particularly draws you, check in with the physical sensations of your head or eyes, your chest, your belly, your pelvis and legs. Give yourself plenty of time to contact these sensations and plenty of time to find some words that seem to fit in describing and articulating them.

If there is time in this inquiry, also give yourself time to see if you can notice the subtler felt sense. If not, you can try this in a later inquiry. Start with simple discriminations. Maybe you can tell—in general or in particular parts of your body—if you feel open or closed, dull or bright, heavy or light. Trust whatever seems to be coming up for you and see how it unfolds. Here more than ever, it can be useful to just take some time and hang out sensing yourself and allowing your breath to help you sense.

Question and Answer: The Felt Sense

I'm having this really weird experience of not being able to sense my head at all. It's like the top of my head is totally missing. Eek!

Isn't that fascinating? How is it when you feel the top of your head missing? Does it seem to be a problem? You can check in a mirror to see that it is still there on your body, if it helps! The main thing to note is that you simply don't *experience* it in the usual way. So . . . sense into the absence, into the emptiness, and let yourself explore it. What is there where your head was? Does it feel empty? . . . clear? . . . dark? . . . Is there something in it? . . . How big is the space? . . . How does it affect you when you are in touch with this? . . . Where does your normal sense of your body start again, and what is happening there? So these are all the kinds of questions you might get curious about when you find some part of your body missing.

Sometimes it may feel like there is a very distinct hole in some part of your body or that some part is missing, like your head, heart, or legs. There may be various kinds of feelings that come with the experience. All of this is just like everything else in the inner world: fascinating experiences to explore! It means you are definitely stepping off the usual and familiar ways of experiencing your body and starting to experience your consciousness in a different way. As you explore, you will see that every experience is meaningful and part of the unfolding of your consciousness and your process.

I'm sensing a pain in my chest and I've been inquiring into it, and it is fairly persistent. I'm not sure if it's something medical to get checked out or whether it is something in my process to allow and explore.

If you sense something in your body that could be a medical condition, it is wise to get it checked out by a medical professional. Inquiry is no substitute for medical care. It is true that sometimes things that arise in our process can influence the health of our bodies. Healing benefits sometimes come about, but they are a by-product of understanding yourself and your truth more clearly, and allowing yourself to function more naturally. They are not the aim of inquiry nor something it promises. If the pain in your chest, or anywhere else, is purely related to your process, then that will become apparent and it will open up in various ways as you explore. But when in doubt, get it checked.

CONCLUSION

BRINGING IT ALL TOGETHER

In this book, you have been steadily learning what it means to get in touch with your experience and to explore it to get clearer and dive deeper. As I said at the beginning, there is no fixed formula for inquiry. It is both an art and a science. And more than that, it is a beautiful way of being that you can cultivate with practice. Each chapter in this book has looked at a particular element of the practice, and as you become more and more familiar with these elements, they will be woven together in your inquiry. It is just like diving: sometimes you are swimming strongly against a current to get to a cave; another time you are holding yourself still so as not to frighten away a creature you are watching, then you have to do a funny maneuver to wiggle around a barrier; sometimes you are drawing in close to inspect the specific markings on the coral to know what it is, and sometimes you are simply speechless in wonder as you just hang loose and take it all in.

Here is a summary of some of the key elements that you have in your tool kit. They have been presented in a general sequence that has a certain sense to it, but in a live exploration, in each moment you can find whichever one fits best with where you are then.

Under each heading, I list a couple of questions that express the particular element. You have seen that a question is a way of being with your experience with curiosity. It is a particular angle of contemplation that invites things to be revealed, just like shining a light in a particular way to see what is there. It is not a demand to think about the right answer. The question helps you discover simply what is true for you: whatever it is that you can actually tell from your immediate experience as you are having it.

In giving several questions for each element, the idea is not that you should run through that list and ask yourself all those questions. They are simply different ways of asking the same kind of thing, and you might find one or two resonate more than others or resonate more in a given moment or situation. In time, you may simply find your own questions.

FRIENDLY CURIOSITY

You started taking a friendly and interested approach to your inner world—the sort that inquiry requires. At any time, with any experience, you can always ask yourself something like:

Am I friendly and open with myself in this moment?
Am I curious about this experience?
What limits my friendliness with myself and my
    experience now?
What is right about not being simply interested in my
    experience?

SENSING, LOOKING, AND LISTENING

You learned how to enter the immediate sensations of the inner world by sensing, looking, and listening. You saw later how the practice of sensing, looking, and listening provides the essential grounding and container for when other elements of your experience get intense—for example, when your mind gets whipped up or very strong feelings emerge. At any point during your inquiry, you can always take a moment to pause, to sense your arms and legs, to look, and to listen. It is not exactly a question, but it helps you ground yourself as you are exploring.

CHECKING IN

You then learned to check in—to look around your inner world and be open to wherever you are and whatever you find. You contemplate your experience with the attitude of questions that help you locate yourself or your experience:

What is here?
Where am I?
What's up with me?
What's going on?

You saw that there are four layers to check in with:

the relevant life or external circumstances, the context
your mind, including your thoughts, ideas, images,
    concepts, beliefs, and the sense of your awareness and
    consciousness
your heart, including your feelings and the emotional or
    affective sense of your experience
your sensations, including your bodily sensations
    and impulses and the inner felt sense of your
    experience

You learned that inquiry means pressing pause on the action of the outer circumstances so that you can dive deeply. You can make this explicit by asking questions such as the following and then focusing on the feelings, thoughts, and sensations:

If *that* is what is going on *around* me (in my
   circumstances), *what* is arising *within* me to meet that?
When that is my situation, what happens inside me?

FINDING A FOCUS

You then learned that once you discover where you are, you find an element or aspect in your experience to explore with questions such as:

What am I interested in?
What draws me?
What is the main thing here?
What am I curious about?
What seems important to look at?
What don't I know here?

THE WHAT

As the focus of your curiosity emerges, you can then begin to explore more about *what* it is. This applies to any of the four layers of your experience.

What *is* this?
What is going on here?
What is this like for me?
What am I experiencing here?

How do I experience that?

Let me see/feel/sense this more . . .

Let me take some breaths into this experience and see
what else I discover about it.

THE WHY

As you begin to experience and discriminate more of what is there, you might also begin to ponder the *why*. Remember that the why is not a theory about what is happening but rather the emerging meanings and causes that you discover and feel are true, directly within your own experience. They get revealed within the experience itself. Here are some helpful questions you might ask:

How come this is here?

What is making this happen?

What's this about?

Why this (of all things)?

You have learned to take every experience you have seriously, to treat it as legitimate and meaningful, but not to take it just at face value: you explore and question it to dive more deeply into where it is coming from inside you.

THE INNER CRITIC/LIFEGUARD

You have seen that inquiry brings a profound freedom to be completely open to whatever might show up in your inner ocean, and you have begun to see how your inner critic limits the scope of your inner world and your exploration. As you are present with any experience, you can check for the presence of the inner critic by asking:

Is this OK with me?

Am I OK to be experiencing this?

Does some part of me think or feel that this shouldn't be
here?

Should I be experiencing something else?

The inner critic tries to push you away from what is actually
true. If you feel OK being with whatever is there in your experience, whatever it may be, then the inner critic has probably not
"got" you, even if you are aware of some slightly critical messages
or some of your own preferences. If you feel it takes you away
from your experience and undermines your ability to stay with
where you are, then it has "got" you. At some point, it will be
useful to disengage—for example, by telling it to get lost and to
let you be with your experience without its interference.

THE MAGIC

The transformational magic of inquiry works by bringing whatever you need as you really get more in touch and clearer about
what is happening in your inner world. You can give the magic
time to happen after something has emerged or been articulated
by contemplating questions such as:

How do I feel about this?

How is this for me?

How is it for me to see this? (Or feel this? Or be in
touch with this? Or be in this situation?)

How does this affect me?

How do I feel toward this part of my experience?

How do my circumstances (or the particular situation)
seem now, after the inquiry?

What changes for me?
What is different for me now?

THE HEAD

Finally, you have begun exploring in a bit more detail the vast realms of the three centers. The head center encompasses the ideas, thoughts, and beliefs that arise in your inner world. You can bring this more into focus by being curious about:

What do I think about this?
What ideas or beliefs do I have about this experience?
How have I experienced this before?
What *don't* I know in this experience?
What if I try to be as clear and discriminating as I can be
    about this experience in the moment?

THE HEART

The heart center is the realm of feeling, affect, and emotion, and helpful questions might include:

What do I feel with or in this experience?
Is the feeling positive or negative? Strong or faint?
What kind of positive, or what kind of negative?
Let me stay with this feeling, breathe into this feeling,
    and see what else I can say about it.
How would I fully express this feeling, consciously and
    in a safe, contained place?

THE BELLY

The belly center concerns embodiment, being in reality, and the subtler sensations of presence itself. Here you might contemplate:

What do I sense in my body with this experience?

How do I experience that in my body or in my consciousness?

What does my body want to do as I'm experiencing this?

What are the sensations that come with this experience?

What is the quality of these sensations? How do they make me feel?

How do I sense my inner state right now?

What is the texture of this experience?

Inquiry takes practice—there really is no shortcut. It is only through practice over the years that you will discover how the various elements weave together: getting in touch, discriminating, articulating, exploring, and questioning to discover and unfold the truth inside you. At the beginning, it can feel like a bit of a slog: not knowing what to do; swimming around feeling a bit lost, mystified, or stumped by what you are finding; thinking you have got it, only to discover that you have not; constantly feeling the need to check with the guidebook or someone else. Often what you encounter might not be easy to be with and to explore because inquiry will always bring you to the edge of your comfort zone. It naturally and powerfully expands your known world toward the unknown. But this is the thrill of the adventure, the endless joy of discovering yourself and your potential, of discovering that which is most satisfying and real for you.

In time, you may realize that it is simply your own presence, your own friendly, curious, and open beingness right there in the immediacy of your own experience that guides and directs your inquiry. One day it may even feel like the very consciousness and beingness of the whole universe itself, unfolding and revealing its magical potentials in your personal life through this play of gradual learning, unfolding, discovery, and revelation.

As you come to the end of this chapter and this book, take a moment once again to come into the immediacy of your experience, noticing what is here right now: sensing, looking, listening . . . noticing what you are feeling in this very moment . . . how your mind is . . . what you sense in your body . . . how it has affected you to engage with this material.

The inner ocean is always right here.

ACKNOWLEDGMENTS

Several people have helped me bring this project to fruition. I am immensely grateful to Hameed Ali and Karen Johnson for the opportunity to develop my initial concept of a basic book on inquiry into an inquiry course for a meditation app. The idea had been germinating for some time, and they were catalytic in getting things moving.

My thanks to Karen for many meetings and discussions of the material as it was developing, and to Hameed for his encouragement, review, and foreword.

Doriena Wolff was an encouraging discussion partner early on in the process.

Zarina Maiwandi very helpfully edited the course version of this material.

My sister Briony Liber and my dear friends Stuart Baillie and Edward Burke read through the material and gave much useful feedback.

Christoph Scaife endured days of home recording studios in the living room as the material was being prepared, and who listened to me bouncing ideas around.

Byron Brown was instrumental in connecting me with Shambhala.

Liz Shaw at Shambhala put her finger on precisely what was missing from the first draft with a question about questions, which led to a great improvement in the practical usefulness of the book.

Thanks to all at Shambhala who engaged in the many aspects of bringing this book into being with such thoughtfulness, thoroughness, and heart.

And lastly, thanks to Sergio Lopez Fernandez, whose enthusiasm for scuba diving sparked the whole metaphor.

RESOURCES

EXPLORING THE UNIVERSE

If you have enjoyed this initial introduction to the practice of diamond inquiry, there are many resources to help you take it further.

WEBSITES

You can visit www.divingintheinnerocean.com to explore a variety of resources related to this book, including courses, meditations, and exercises to help you learn and practice different elements of inquiry. My website, www.domliber.com, has additional resources relating to my work more broadly. And the main Diamond Approach website, www.diamondapproach.org, is the online home of the Ridhwan School (see more below).

BOOKS

The following books are highly recommended:

Spacecruiser Inquiry: True Guidance for the Inner Journey, by A. H. Almaas, is the ultimate manual of diamond inquiry and exploration. You will learn to refine and develop your practice by bringing many different qualities of your essential nature into the practice itself. These include strength, joy, compassion, steadfastness, power, and many others. You will learn to explore not only the more familiar terrain of the inner ocean of this world, so to speak, but also the distant reaches and almost interstellar possibilities that emerge as your exploration expands.

The Unfolding Now: Realizing Your True Nature through the Practice of Presence, by A. H. Almaas, is another very important book that focuses on one specific aspect of inquiry, closely related to what we have called "checking in." It is about being where you are and recognizing where you are as you are being there. In particular, the first nine chapters are an accessible and indispensable exploration of some of the barriers to simply being where you are. As you become conscious of the barriers and how you get in your own way, things naturally begin opening up with the magic of inquiry.

Soul without Shame: A Guide to Liberating Yourself from the Judge Within, by Byron Brown, is a vital resource for dealing with the inner critic or superego: the inner lifeguard that we met in chapter 9. It will help you recognize when the inner critic is active in your inquiry and in your life more broadly. You will be guided through very practical steps to expose and then disengage from its cruel and limiting judgmental attacks.

The Diamond Approach: An Introduction to the Teachings of A. H. Almaas, by John Davis, is a wonderful overview of the broader practice, path, and framework of the Diamond Approach.

RIDHWAN SCHOOL

The Ridhwan School, the home of the Diamond Approach, was established by A. H. Almaas and Karen Johnson to house the teachings and practice of the Diamond Approach, to train teachers, and to make the teaching and method available.

You can contact the school to find a teacher, if that is something you would like to do. Teachers can be helpful in three primary formats. The first is through one-to-one private sessions. If there is teacher close to you, then you might be able to see them in person. And if that is not possible, then you can look at online sessions.

Some teachers also offer group sessions called *small groups* or *inquiry groups*, either in person or online. These are a wonderful way to learn inquiry, because each student gets to practice inquiry under the guidance of the teacher *and* see the teacher working with other students—you see the inquiry process from the outside and can learn more about it that way. When you are doing your own inquiry with the teacher, you are often too deep in the weeds to really learn about the process, whereas the small group gives you a chance to see it one step removed and learn that way.

Finally, some teachers share the teaching in ongoing Diamond Approach groups, in which the full practice and teaching of the path are shared with a larger group of students. These groups can carry on for many years, even decades, without exhausting the journey.

You can find the school online and get connected with a teacher at www.diamondapproach.org. The school's website also has many other useful resources, including a glossary of useful concepts in the Diamond Approach and an overview of the many books that have been written by A. H. Almaas.

DIAMOND APPROACH ONLINE

The online arm of the school has discrete courses, taken on demand and at your own pace, that include: a course on which this book is based; an inner critic course taught by Byron Brown, based on his book *Soul without Shame*; and courses focused on particular elements of life, such as parenting or John Davis's course on life transitions.

Diamond Approach Online, online.diamondapproach.org, also offers online inquiry groups where you meet with up to fourteen other students and a teacher for a small group, as described above. These are offered regularly, and students sign up for a period of three months at a time.

INDEX

ABOUT THE AUTHOR

Dominic C. Liber is a writer, teacher, and explorer of the inner world who has a lifelong fascination with both magic and mystery as well as science and sense. A Diamond Approach student for over twenty years and a Diamond Approach teacher since 2015, he has been on the inner journey and teaching meditation and other practices for over thirty years. A former actuary and social impact investor, Dominic now works entirely with the Diamond Approach, leading groups and working with students mostly in the UK and South Africa. He is passionate about making the extraordinary practice of diamond inquiry accessible, including to many who might not think of themselves as spiritual in any traditional sense. On a daily basis he experiences diamond inquiry as a doorway to an incredible, ongoing journey for himself and for his students. Dominic largely splits his time between London and South Africa—and is almost as enthusiastic about coffee, nature, and dancing as he is about diamond inquiry.